Volleyball

Fourth Edition

Darlene A. Kluka

Grambling State University of Louisiana

Peter J. Dunn

Associate Vice President, Member Relations and Human Resources
Division, USA Volleyball

D0294426

Boston   Burr Ridge, IL   Dubuque, IA   Madison WI
New York   San Francisco   St. Louis
Bangkok   Bogotá   Caracas   Lisbon   London   Madrid   Mexico City
Milan   New Delhi   Seoul   Singapore   Sydney   Taipei   Toronto

McGraw-Hill Higher Education

A Division of The **McGraw-Hill** *Companies*

WINNING EDGE SERIES: VOLLEYBALL, FOURTH EDITION

This book is printed on acid-free paper.

2 3 4 5 6 7 8 9 0 DOC/DOC 0 9 8 7 6 5 4 3 2 1 0

ISBN 0–07–230030–2

Vice president and editorial director: *Kevin T. Kane*
Publisher: *Edward E. Bartell*
Executive editor: *Vicki Malinee*
Developmental editor: *Tricia R. Musel*
Senior marketing manager: *Pamela S. Cooper*
Project manager: *Mary Lee Harms*
Production supervisor: *Laura Fuller*
Coordinator of freelance design: *Michelle D. Whitaker*
Senior photo research coordinator: *Lori Hancock*
Supplement coordinator: *Sandra M. Schnee*
Compositor: *Interactive Composition Corporation*
Typeface: *10/12 Palatino*
Printer: *R. R. Donnelley & Sons Company/Crawfordsville, IN*

Cover image: © *Bill Leslie Photography*

Library of Congress Cataloging-in-Publication Data

Kluka, Darlene A.
    Volleyball / Darlene A. Kluka, Peter J. Dunn.—4th ed.
      p.   cm. — (Winning edge series)
    Includes index.
    ISBN 0–07–230030–2
    1. Volleyball.   I. Dunn, Peter J.   II. Title.   III. Series:
Winning edge series (Boston, Mass.)
GV1015.3.K58   2000
796.325—dc21   99–32562
                                       CIP

www.mhhe.com

DEDICATION

To the memories of my mother, Lillian; my aunt, Annie; my uncle, Alois; and my cousins, Ray and Helen (Emily).   D. A. K.

With thanks to my wife, Kate, for her support.   P. J. D.

CONTENTS

PREFACE

Spectators and players alike can witness or compete on volleyball courts across the world. Whether you play on beach or indoor courts, gather up to 12 players and you have a volleyball game. Volleyball is a sport for any season.

Health professionals keep reporting about the benefits of regular exercise. Volleyball is a great way to accomplish personal fitness and a good way to have fun while getting in shape. If you are one of the players who would like to solve the mysteries of forearm passing, setting, or serving, this is the book for you—it will serve as a road map to better your skills. The presentation is clear and well illustrated.

So read the book and practice the skills. Welcome to a volleyball journey!

▶ Audience

This text is designed for anyone who likes volleyball and plays it, as well as for students in academic courses on volleyball. The book is intended to be an easy-to-read, useful resource tool that provides information about how to develop and improve your skills.

▶ Features

This book starts out by discussing the nomenclature of the game and its special qualities. It includes volleyball indoors and beach game history as well as the opportunities to incorporate volleyball as a lifetime activity. Succeeding chapters address "Facilities and Equipment" and "Rules and Terminology." Together these separate chapters familiarize you with the ease in which the game can be played with limited facilities and equipment, to the evolution of the rules and language used in volleyball. The next seven chapters delve into these specifics of volleyball: overall physical fitness, passing, serving, spiking and blocking, introductory and advanced playing systems, and advanced skills.

After the skill chapters, turn to the numerous appendices that list officiating signals, additional resources, visual exercises, and an USA volleyball organizational chart. The thorough glossary at the back of the book will help you with any terms you might find unfamiliar.

Special features that further enhance this book include:

- Each chapter opens with a list of objectives and closes with a bulleted summary to reinforce the major points covered.
- Key terms are highlighted in boldface type in the text and are defined on the page at the point of use. This feature enables you to build a working vocabulary on concepts and principles necessary for beginning, developing, and maintaining your skills.

- Checklist boxes outline techniques, applications, and strategies for quick review.

▶ Acknowledgements

The fourth edition of this book has been completed with passion for a sport that provides those who play it with an insight into their souls. Many others are also involved in that passion. Some contribute the tangibles: figures, diagrams, and words. An expression of thanks is extended to Pete Dunn, Tricia Musel, and the staff of McGraw-Hill for facilitating this portion. Others contribute ideas, philosophy, beliefs, nurturing, and support. Marilyn McReavy Nolen, Mary Jo Peppler, Ruth Nelson, Barbara Viera, Dr. Geri Polvino, and John Kessel have nurtured my interest as a student of the game of volleyball; Dr. Taras Liskevych, Dr. Doug Beal, Bob Gambardella, Dr. Cecile Reynaud, Debbie Hunter, and Sandy Vivas have helped me understand the importance of philosophy and its incorporation into the game and its programs; Drs. Aileene Lockhart and Jane Mott have believed in my ability as a teacher/coach/mentor. Additionally, Dr. Karen Johnson and Susan True have helped me gain additional perspective of the history of the game for women. Dr. Don Shondell and Al Monaco have provided me with additional insight into the history of the men's game, while Dale Hoffman has provided insight into the beach game.

Still others have provided inspiration. Dr. Jonathan Reeser and Ken Kontor have provided me with a more complete understanding of the significance of sports medicine within volleyball; Dr. Martha Ludwig and Dr. Linda Bunker have supported my commitment to sport science through volleyball. Special appreciation is offered to faculty and staff at Grambling State University: Dr. Willie Daniel, Dr. Martin Ayim, Dr. Faye Avard, Dr. Jeanette Hutchinson, Dr. Obadiah Simmons, Dr. Robert Lyons, Barbara Lewis, Dorcia Chaison, Anna Reed, Andrea Taylor, Fred Collins, Terry Lilly, Dr. Dorothy Hardy, Dr. Phyllis Love, Sheila Griffin, and Berfina Ridgell, for serving as the "wind beneath my wings" so that I could find the time to complete this edition.

The photographs for this text have been contributed by a variety of individuals. Each has been credited beneath each photo. The creative capturing of the game through the camera's eye by all those involved is appreciated.

We would like to thank the following reviewers, who provided us with expert commentary during the development of this edition:

- Tammy Saboorin, Valencia Community College
- Xiao J. Li, Adirondack Community College
- Heldi Funne Shah, University of Louisville
- Ruchelle Dunwoody, Miami University (Ohio)
- Hilda Fronske, Utah State University
- Suzanne Seares, El Camino College

Each of us has made a small contribution to the sport of volleyball. Collectively, we touch all those who are and will be students of the game.

D. A. K.

CHAPTER 1

WHAT IS VOLLEYBALL ALL ABOUT?

OBJECTIVES

After reading this chapter, you should be able to do the following:

* Verbally recount a history of indoor and beach volleyball games.
* Recognize the role of sport governance in the game around the world.
* Understand why volleyball is considered a game for lifetime, and the ways it can be adapted to fit the needs of individuals throughout life.

KEY TERMS

While reading this chapter, you will become familiar with the following terms:

► rotational order (serving order)
► spikers (hitters, attackers)
► blockers

► backs
► overlap
► points
► sideout

Continued on p. 2.

1

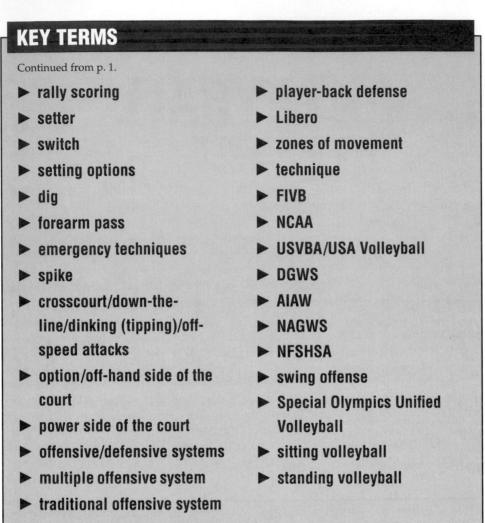

KEY TERMS

Continued from p. 1.

- ▶ rally scoring
- ▶ setter
- ▶ switch
- ▶ setting options
- ▶ dig
- ▶ forearm pass
- ▶ emergency techniques
- ▶ spike
- ▶ crosscourt/down-the-line/dinking (tipping)/off-speed attacks
- ▶ option/off-hand side of the court
- ▶ power side of the court
- ▶ offensive/defensive systems
- ▶ multiple offensive system
- ▶ traditional offensive system

- ▶ player-back defense
- ▶ Libero
- ▶ zones of movement
- ▶ technique
- ▶ FIVB
- ▶ NCAA
- ▶ USVBA/USA Volleyball
- ▶ DGWS
- ▶ AIAW
- ▶ NAGWS
- ▶ NFSHSA
- ▶ swing offense
- ▶ Special Olympics Unified Volleyball
- ▶ sitting volleyball
- ▶ standing volleyball

By its nature, the game of volleyball requires cooperation and communication. A team's success not only depends upon individual skill and effort but also upon the total contribution of each individual's effort to overall team performance. A true team is composed of individuals who ultimately understand the language of the game.

A volleyball team consists of six players. They are arranged in a **rotational order** at the time of service **(serving order)**, with three players in the back court and three in the front court. The three players in the front court are considered potential **spikers (hitters** or **attackers on offense**—left, middle, and right—or **blockers on defense)**; the three back court players are referred to as **backs** (left, middle, and right).

No player may completely **overlap** (extend over and cover a part of) the court area of an adjacent player (a player who is directly in front, in back, or to either side) at the time of service. Position is determined by the placement of the feet as the ball is contacted by the server. Once the ball has been served, players may move freely anywhere on their side of the court. The objective is to make the ball hit the floor on the opponents' side of the court or prevent its return to one's own side of the court. Before rally scoring, **points** are scored when the receiving team does not successfully return the ball. A **sideout** is awarded if the serving team cannot successfully return the ball. In **rally scoring,** each rally wins a point whether it is won by the serving or receiving team. Most frequently, a **setter** will move and hitters will change places, or **switch,** in the front court to create offensively advantageous situations. The setter may overhand pass (set) or back pass (back set) to hitters, using a variety of **setting options** (short, medium, or high outside). Those considered to be back court players generally use a **dig** (a forearm pass in a low movement zone to get a play on a hard-driven hit) or a **forearm pass** to play the ball (as the ball cannot be visibly held or thrown). It may also be necessary for the back court players to employ **emergency techniques** (dives and rolls) to play a ball that has been hit hard, sharply angled, or tipped over the block by the opposing attack. Occasionally, it may be advantageous for a back court player to **spike** the ball. Back court players may spike only if they take off from behind the 3 m attack line on the court. If they are on or in front of the attack line, they may not play the ball if it is completely above the top level of the net.

During play, a hitter has the options of spiking the ball across the court **(cross-court)** or **down the line, dinking (tipping)** the ball over the block, or hitting an **off-speed** shot into the opponents' court. The attacker may hit the ball from the **option** (off-hand) **side** of the court or prefer to hit from the **power side.** The left front (LF) is an example of a right-handed attacker's power side; option side means that the ball is contacted after it crosses in front of the attacker's body.

Each team has the opportunity to play offensively and defensively. It is only logical that **offensive** and **defensive systems** be created by each team. The offensive system used by a team is determined by the skill and maturity levels of the players as well as the desired outcome from use of the system. If the team uses a three-player attack, bringing a setter from the back court, the attack is considered a **multiple offensive system** (6-2; 5-1). When the team uses a two-hitter attack, the attack is considered a **traditional offensive system** (4-2).

Defensively, vulnerability of areas on the court will determine the type of system used per play. If the center of the court is most susceptible to the attack, a **player-up defense** is employed. If the attack is hitting the ball deeply into the back court, the team may choose to use a **player-back defense.**

The **Libero** position is filled by a defensive specialist who is free to substitute any time the ball is dead and does not need to report to the second referee. The Libero cannot serve, attack (when the ball is above the height of the net), block, or overhand set in front of the attack line. When the Libero is removed from the game, one rally must pass before a Libero may reenter the game. The Libero must wear a uniform contrasting in color to that of the team's.

SPECIAL QUALITIES OF THE GAME

Many games played by Americans are possession sports. Football, soccer, field hockey, and basketball have rules and strategies that allow each team to control the ball for extended periods of time. One statistic kept for these sports is "time of possession" of the ball for each team.

Volleyball, however, is a game of rebound and movement. The ball is never motionless from the moment it is served until it contacts the floor or is whistled dead by an official. Winning the game is determined by points.

The size of the court is relatively small for the number of players, creating a congested playing area. Because of this, the game has evolved into one of efficiency, accuracy, and supportive movements. Each team has a maximum of three contacts with which to accomplish the game's objective, which is to return the ball and have it contact the floor on the opponents' side of the net within the boundaries of their court. The outcome of the rally, game, and match becomes a summation of each player's efforts. This is the ultimate in individual contribution and team effort.

Substitutions are limited, encouraging versatility among players. Because player rotation is a mandatory part of the game, each player experiences up to six different orientations, three in the back court and three in the front court. Time-outs are brief, creating the potential for dramatic shifts in momentum. These shifts in momentum help make the game of volleyball constantly dynamic and continuously intriguing.

Volleyball is a team sport which uses a net to create no intentional physical contact between opposing teams. Reaching over the net into the opponents' court is permitted during the follow-through motion of the attacker's arm after the ball has been hit, or in the act of blocking after the hitter has contacted the ball.

FIGURE 1-1 A forearm pass in a low movement zone. Courtesy of D. Kluka.

The individual techniques of the game are quite different from those of most team sports. Because the essence of the game requires the body to move through all **zones of movement** (airborne, high, medium, low), the ball can be played at the highest point of a jump or just inches from the floor. The forearm pass is one technique unique to the game. No other team sport fosters ball-to-forearm contact as an accurate and efficient skill.

Techniques have evolved as a direct result of the rules that govern the game. The quality of the administrator of those rules, the referee, may determine the level of skill acceptable to play a successful match (three out of five games). The acceptability of *each* contact is interpreted by the official. Volleyball **technique,** or how the ball is played, is a primary ingredient of the game. Court size, number of players, the number of contacts permitted, and ball speeds (ranging from less than one mile per hour to in excess of one hundred miles per hour) contribute to the excitement and popularity of the game of volleyball for both players and spectators.

APPAREL

The volleyball "brief " was developed for women to cover the hip region and buttocks when executing dives, rolls, and other emergency techniques. Briefs have been available in nylon/Lycra blends and cotton/polyester blends. The major disadvantage in the brief is its inability to adequately cover the thigh area to prevent floor burns. Men have opted to wear shorts or half-sweats. The popularity of shorts has recurred, and they are long enough to cover the thigh area.

Short- or long-sleeved shirts have also been worn to absorb perspiration and reduce abrasions. Screened logos often appear on the back of the shirt to prevent sticking when players dive or sprawl while performing emergency techniques.

Beach volleyball shorts have been made from Lycra or Spandex. Men's shirts have been made of a cotton/polyester and are usually tank tops. Many female players have worn jogging bra tops for comfort and support.

Appropriate shoes for indoor play are extremely lightweight with added cushioning in the inner and outer soles. The cushioning helps dissipate force throughout the foot rather than through the foot to the leg. Because movements in volleyball include jumping, changing directions quickly, and continuous flow from service to the end of each rally, nylon mesh and leather uppers comprise the basis of the shoe to reduce shoe weight. The sole is flat to assist in stability of the foot as well as to prevent ankle injuries. Finally, good ankle, arch, and heel supports are important when considering volleyball shoe durability.

In late 1998, in cooperation with international sporting goods manufacturers, Federation Internationale de Volleyball **(FIVB)** developed new standards for uniforms. The purpose of the change was to elicit a new image to volleyball by creating a more revealing body line. In general, baggy or loose uniforms are no longer permitted. Shirts and shorts must follow the body line; women may wear one-piece uniforms. Long-sleeve shirts are also prohibited. Numbers are worn on the rightside leg of the shorts; the country flag and country name is on the left, front side of the shirt; each player's last name is on the back of the shirt, above the number.

Knee pads are an optional part of the volleyball uniform for indoor play. Because the surfaces of gymnasiums have little flexibility, it is suggested that knee protection be worn, particularly while learning. Knee pads that provide cushioning to the anterior surface of the joint from approximately two inches above to two inches below the knee should be considered when purchasing.

HISTORY OF THE INDOOR GAME

William G. Morgan, the physical director of the Holyoke, Massachusetts, Young Men's Christian Association (YMCA), created a game called Mintonette in 1895. It was initially devised as a less strenuous activity than basketball for middle-aged businessmen who attended YMCA classes (see Appendix E for original rules). The game incorporated baseball, handball, and tennis-related skills. The objective was to hit the ball back and forth with the hands. Each team, having any number of players, was permitted three outs before the team forfeited the ball.

Because the basic idea of play was to bat the ball with the hands back and forth over a net, the game was renamed "volleyball" in 1896. Earliest rules mandated the game be played in nine innings on a 25' × 50' court. The serve was hit over a 6'6" net; it could be assisted by any offensive player. The bladder of a basketball was originally used for the ball, but it was too light. A basketball was too heavy. A. G. Spalding (later of Spalding Sporting Goods Company) constructed a ball expressly for the game.

Touching the net during a point attempt was illegal. The ball could be dribbled within four feet of the net. By 1900, the concepts of innings and dribbling were eliminated; nets were seven feet high, substantially shorter than the ones used in men's and women's volleyball today.

Twelve years later, the YMCA formed a special committee which developed major rule modifications and standardized ball handling. The court was enlarged to 35' × 60'; the net was raised to 7'6"; serve rotation of players was incorporated, and the two-out-of-three game match was established. The YMCA used the new rules in the first Open Invitational Tournament held in Germantown, Pennsylvania. Players called their own fouls. In 1916, the YMCA, in conjunction with the National Collegiate Athletic Association (**NCAA**), published men's rules. The net was elevated to 8'; the game was concluded at 15 points.

During the early 1900s, the YMCA exerted the greatest influence upon the growth and development of volleyball. The game was introduced in Canada and in Central and South America by YMCA missionaries. In 1913, it was included in the Far Eastern Games in Manila, Philippine Islands; by 1914, it was being played in England and Europe. During World War I, the American Expeditionary Forces distributed over sixteen thousand volleyballs to their troops and allies in Western Europe. Immediately after the war, several Eastern European nations adopted the game and rapidly began national competitions.

The 1920s was the decade of most rapid change for volleyball in the United States. The first men's YMCA National Championships were held in 1922 at the Brooklyn Central YMCA. The National Amateur Athletic Federation (**NAAF**)—later the Amateur Athletic Union (**AAU**) sanctioned volleyball as an official national activity in 1923. In 1924, the first intramural volleyball program was instituted at the University of Illinois. That same year, the first interscholastic (high school) volleyball program was founded in Pittsburgh, Pennsylvania.

Special rules were published for girls and women in the Red Cover Series of the Spalding Athletic Library. Additionally, the National Section on Women's Athletics (NSWA), a division of the American Physical Education Association (APEA), created a totally independent set of rules for females. These rules, instituted in 1926, closely resemble those being used today. Court dimensions were restructured to 30' × 60', the ball could be contacted legally above the waist only, and no more than three contacts per side were permitted.

In 1928, for the purpose of regulating the rules nationally and to create a national open championship, the United States Volleyball Association **(USVBA)** was formed. National championships were contested in a joint USVBA/YMCA tournament in three men's divisions: an open, a veterans (now called senior), and a YMCA.

During the 1930s, NSWA had changed its name to the National Section for Girls' and Women's Sports **(NSGWS)** and had published a separate rules book for girls and women. The rules were used at the high school and college levels in volleyball classes and intramural competitions.

The ten years prior to World War II were relatively stable ones for volleyball, with few changes in rules or play. The University of Washington formed the first men's varsity volleyball program with awards in 1934. The state of Pennsylvania sanctioned the first boys' high school championships in 1938.

American armed forces stationed in the South Pacific during World War II found the game of volleyball a relaxing alternative to fervent fighting in the jungles and on the beaches. A rope, strewn with seaweed, was strung between two trees to serve as a net. The game spread among the people of the islands occupied by American troops. The Japanese, in particular, developed a keen interest and flair for the game.

During the five years after the war, several advancements occurred internationally. In 1946, college club teams developed all over the United States as war veterans, who had played during the war, returned to college. The FIVB was established in 1947 with fourteen member nations to serve as the official international governing body for the sport. In 1948, the first European Championships were held in Rome. The first college in the nation to offer men's scholarships in volleyball and have a full-time coach was Florida State University in 1949. The USVBA, in the same year, added a women's division to its national Open Championships.

NSGWS became the Division for Girls' and Women's Sports **(DGWS)** in 1958. It published guides that included rules which were recognized as official for girls and women. Each guide included rules, standards, officiating instructions, and professionally written teaching/coaching articles.

During the two decades following the Korean conflict, the USVBA began its surge of national leadership in the amateur sport of volleyball. In 1952, the USVBA sponsored a men's team at the second World Championships and also sent a team to the first World Championships for women. From 1952 to 1964, it sanctioned the men's National Armed Forces Championships; it instituted the men's National Collegiate Championships and was involved with them until 1969; it helped sponsor a men's team to the first Pan-American Championships in 1955; and it assisted in sending men's and women's teams to the Olympic Games in 1964.

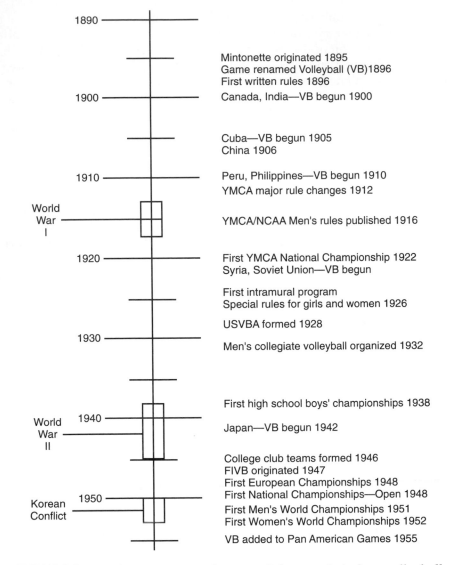

1890 ——

Mintonette originated 1895
Game renamed Volleyball (VB)1896
First written rules 1896
1900 —— Canada, India—VB begun 1900

Cuba—VB begun 1905
China 1906

1910 —— Peru, Philippines—VB begun 1910
YMCA major rule changes 1912

World
War —— YMCA/NCAA Men's rules published 1916
I

1920 —— First YMCA National Championship 1922
Syria, Soviet Union—VB begun

First intramural program
Special rules for girls and women 1926

USVBA formed 1928

1930 ——
Men's collegiate volleyball organized 1932

First high school boys' championships 1938

World   1940
War —— Japan—VB begun 1942
II

College club teams formed 1946
FIVB originated 1947
First European Championships 1948
First National Championships—Open 1948
1950 ——
Korean   First Men's World Championships 1951
Conflict   First Women's World Championships 1952

VB added to Pan American Games 1955

FIGURE 1-2 Significant events and accomplishments in indoor volleyball.

Although volleyball had its roots in the United States, it was not played as competitively in the United States as in Japan, Cuba, China, or the Soviet Union. When the 1964 Olympic Games were held in Tokyo, volleyball was initiated as an Olympic sport for men and women. It was one of three trial sports introduced by the host nation. The Japanese style of play revolutionized and helped develop the game into one of power, agility, endurance, and finesse. Additionally, the texture and size of the ball were altered to make it faster and more difficult to manipulate. Ball handling interpretations by officials were also adapted to assist the style of play.

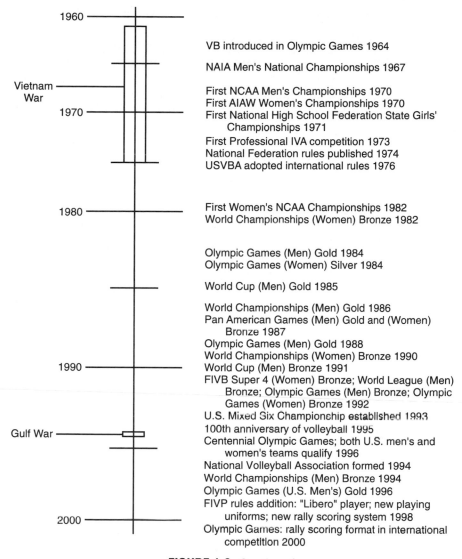

1960	
	VB introduced in Olympic Games 1964
	NAIA Men's National Championships 1967
Vietnam War	First NCAA Men's Championships 1970
	First AIAW Women's Championships 1970
1970	First National High School Federation State Girls' Championships 1971
	First Professional IVA competition 1973
	National Federation rules published 1974
	USVBA adopted international rules 1976
1980	First Women's NCAA Championships 1982
	World Championships (Women) Bronze 1982
	Olympic Games (Men) Gold 1984
	Olympic Games (Women) Silver 1984
	World Cup (Men) Gold 1985
	World Championships (Men) Gold 1986
	Pan American Games (Men) Gold and (Women) Bronze 1987
	Olympic Games (Men) Gold 1988
	World Championships (Women) Bronze 1990
1990	World Cup (Men) Bronze 1991
	FIVB Super 4 (Women) Bronze; World League (Men) Bronze; Olympic Games (Men) Bronze; Olympic Games (Women) Bronze 1992
	U.S. Mixed Six Championship established 1993
Gulf War	100th anniversary of volleyball 1995
	Centennial Olympic Games; both U.S. men's and women's teams qualify 1996
	National Volleyball Association formed 1994
	World Championships (Men) Bronze 1994
	Olympic Games (U.S. Men's) Gold 1996
	FIVP rules addition: "Libero" player; new playing uniforms; new rally scoring system 1998
2000	Olympic Games: rally scoring format in international competition 2000

FIGURE 1-2 *Continued.*

Women's involvement in the game of volleyball rapidly increased after World War II. After the first women's USVBA National Championship (1949) and the first World Championships for women (1952), the Women's Athletic Division of the American Association for Health, Physical Education, and Recreation (AAHPER) revised its rules to coincide with the women's rules of USVBA.

Women served as head coaches for the U.S. women's Olympic volleyball team in the 1964 and 1968 Olympic Games. Jane Ward, at the 1968 Olympic Games in Mexico City, served as the last female head coach for any U.S. Olympic volleyball team to date. Males have served as head coaches for every men's Olympic volleyball team to date.

Volleyball also grew at the high school level, particularly for girls. In 1971, fourteen states hosted state high school championships for girls and six for boys (boys championships began in 1938).

Volleyball gained enough popularity by the early 1970s to justify the development of the first professional volleyball competition in the western United States. An organization known as the International Professional Volleyball League was also formed. Professional volleyball disappeared within a few years, because of lack of funding. A decade later, another effort to start a professional volleyball league was initiated in the United States.

The NCAA continued the men's collegiate championship series by sponsoring the first NCAA Championship in 1970. The Association of Interscholastic Athletics for Women (AIAW) sponsored its first women's national championships in 1970 and continued them until 1981. As a result of the NCAA sponsorship of a women's national championship in 1982 with expenses paid to participating teams, the AIAW lost participants and dropped its own championships.

In 1975, women's volleyball was the first national Olympic program to develop a full-time residency training program, centered in Texas. Players selected for the national team could live, work, and train together for the first time.

Internationally today, the sport of volleyball is controlled and regulated by the FIVB. The federation currently has over 200 member countries. Its national counterpart in the United States, the national governing body, is USA Volleyball, also known as USVBA. The organization adopted international rules in 1976. In addition to USA Volleyball, other national organizations, such as the National Association for Girls and Women in Sport (NAGWS), and the National Federation of State High School Associations (NFSHSA), publish rules and guidelines for play at local, state, regional, and national levels for college and high school competition.

Games called "Doubles" or "Triples" are additional variations played. A doubles team consists of two players; a triples team is composed of three. Each team's court is shorter than the six-player court. Individual techniques may differ slightly because of varying zones of responsibility on the court.

Coed play (males and females on the same team) gained popularity with the advent of Title IX legislation in the 1970s. Its roots branched from the West Coast eastward. Serving order alternates one female and one male on the court. If the ball is played more than once per side, one contact must be made by a female. Other rule modifications have been incorporated to make the game challenging and exciting for players and spectators. The Mixed Six National Championships were established in 1993.

The roots of the game of volleyball are deeply woven into the history of the United States, with periods of war boosting its popularity. Competitively, its branches blossomed in foreign countries such as Japan, Cuba, and the Soviet Union. Not until the 1984 Olympic Games had the roots developed sufficiently to bear fruit once again in the United States.

After the success of the men's and women's Olympic volleyball teams, the U.S. men's and women's national teams consolidated their programs with a national training center located in San Diego, California. This provided the opportunity for cooperative training and leadership efforts for all individuals involved in competitive programs at the national and international levels.

In the 1980s, the U.S. men's teams won the 1985 World Cup and the 1986 World Championships. This marked the first time in history that the U.S. men's team had won the "Triple Crown" of volleyball (the Olympics, the World Cup, and the World Championships) in consecutive years (1984, 1985, 1986).

The United States, by the end of the 1980s, had established itself as a world volleyball power. Many believe the primary contributing factors included a full-time training center and a unique style of play. By studying American characteristics and philosophy, members of the national training center staff created an approach to the game that was uniquely "American." It involved a **swing offense,** based upon an attack from the inside working out, and a defense that combined agility with power.

At the high school level in 1999, girls' volleyball was ranked third in participation (after basketball and track and field), with more than 320,000 girls at 12,240 schools participating. From 1988 to 1992, the National Federation of State High School Associations recorded 22,624 boys participating at 1,122 schools. The participation figures nearly doubled in the four-year period.

In 1993, volleyball was the second most popular sport (40%) played at Sportsplex Owners and Directors of America (SODA) facilities, with 33% of its member facilities having volleyball programs. SODA recorded nearly 150,000 people using each sportsplex facility during 1993.

FIGURE 1-3 One of the greatest women to play the indoor game: Flo Hyman. Courtesy of USA Volleyball.

FIGURE 1-4 One of the greatest men to play the indoor and beach games: Karch Kiraly (USA-#15). Courtesy of USA Volleyball.

In 1994, women's volleyball programs at NCAA member schools were conducted by almost 800 institutions and involved more than 10,000 women student/athletes. Similarly, men's volleyball programs were conducted at over 60 institutions, providing intercollegiate opportunities for more than 1,000 men.

By 1998, American Sports Data Corporation (ASDC) determined that 41.3 million people considered themselves participants in volleyball, 28 million in the indoor and outdoor grass, and 13.3 million in beach and/or sand outdoors. This made volleyball the number two most participated sport in the world, just behind basketball (at 47 million), and ahead of softball at 27 million and soccer at 18 million.

According to American Volleyball Coaches Association (AVCA) figures, the NCAA Division I, II, and III levels offering women's volleyball programs in 1998 included 927 schools; those offering men's volleyball programs included 75 schools.

By 1998, the National Federation of State High School Associations (NFSHA) released impressive figures. Those high schools offering girls' varsity volleyball programs rose to 12,957, while those offering boys' programs catapulted to 1,441. Actual female participants elevated to 370,957. Actual male participants blossomed to 32,375.

The National Volleyball Association (NVA) was created in 1994 to promote the indoor women's game and provide opportunities for professional play throughout the United States. Those who dominated play during the 1990s include Lori Endicott, Tara Cross-Battle, Caren Kemner, Teee Williams, Yoko Zetterland-Bush, Tammy Liley, Danielle Scott, Natalie Williams, Marissa Hatchet, Elaina Oden, Bev Oden, Gabrielle Reece, and Deitre Collins.

The involvement of USA Volleyball (a.k.a. USVBA—United States Volleyball Association) during the decade of the 1990s was evidenced from the highest level of international competition (U.S.A. men's and women's teams), to U.S. Junior Olympic Volleyball Championships, to grassroots competition through USA Volleyball regions and member organizations. USA Volleyball also conducts national programs in Coaching Education (CAP), U.S.A. Youth Volleyball, U.S. Open Volleyball, and U.S. Club Championships. Additionally, USA Volleyball establishes rules and certifies national and international officials. There are more than thirty USA Volleyball regions covering fifty states and U.S. Commonwealths. USA Volleyball also is affiliated with 33 member organizations such as the YMCA, NCAA, Armed Forces, and AAHPERD, which represents more than three million players. As the National Governing Body (NGB) for the sport, USA Volleyball has taken a leadership role in the development of the indoor and outdoor games of volleyball, making it one of the largest and fastest growing grassroots participation sports in the United States. Additional details about how you can become involved in volleyball as a player, coach, or administrator can be found in Appendices B and D.

INDOOR VOLLEYBALL AND SPECIAL POPULATIONS

Volleyball is presently played at least once a week by more than 800 million people in 210 countries. This participation generates annual business of $6.5 billion dollars, just over 5% of the overall world expenditures in sport participation. The sport also attracts hundreds of thousands of spectators and millions of telespectators who support the indoor and outdoor games. Several groups who benefit directly through participation in volleyball are Special Olympics and Disabled Sports. The development of **Special Olympics Unified Volleyball** programs has been a conscious attempt to integrate those athletes with mental disabilities and those who participate as their partners through volleyball. Begun in the mid-1980s through the efforts of Ruth Nelson, a volleyball Olympian (1976) as the first Special Olympics Volleyball Director, skill and game competitions were initiated for Special Olympians. Today, anyone who is interested in playing and/or coaching volleyball competitively and who also has an interest in Special Olympics should inquire with the Special Olympics program in the community. Special Olympic volleyball athletes and their partners participate in local, state, and national competition. Within the United States, Special Olympics Unified Volleyball Championships have been infused into the United States Volleyball National Championships, first entering as an exhibition sport in 1994, then providing national championship level competition since 1996.

In 1956, the Dutch Sports Committee presented the sport of **sitting volleyball** to the world. It was a combination of sitzball, begun in Germany in 1953, and volleyball. Sitting volleyball has evolved to be a highly competitive game for those with and without disabilities. Played on a smaller court and reduced net height, sitting volleyball closely resembles the spirit of the game invented by William G. Morgan in the USA in 1895. The major difference is that players must remain seated while playing the game. It was 1978, however, before the International Sports Organization for the Disabled (ISOD) placed sitting volleyball for men on the official program. By 1980, it was accepted as a Paralympic sport for men. In 1993, championships for women were established.

Standing volleyball was played in Great Britain after World War II by men with disabilities, generally those with amputations. Since 1980, standing volleyball has

FIGURE 1-5 Sitting volleyball demonstration. Courtesy of D. Kluka.

Sitting Volleyball Rules

Court size and net height are modified for sitting volleyball. Most courts are 10 m × 6 m, dividing the court in two equal courts, 5 m × 6 m. The net is 1.15 m high. The attack lines are parallel to the centerline and 2 m from the middle of the centerline.

Players' positions are determined by the positions of their "bottoms" rather than placement of hand or feet on the floor. ("Bottom" refers the player's area from shoulders to buttocks.) Touching with the hand on the court beyond the centerline is permitted as long as there is contact with the centerline. Any other body part contacting the opponent's court is prohibited. Space under the net may be penetrated as long as there is no interference with an opposing player.

Each player's bottom must remain in contact with the floor when contacting the ball on an attack. Back row attacks can be made from any height as long as the player's bottom has not touched or crossed over the attack line during the hit. Some part of the upper body must also remain in contact with the floor at all times, except when making a defensive play or while in the free zone.

Sitting Volleyball Court Diagram

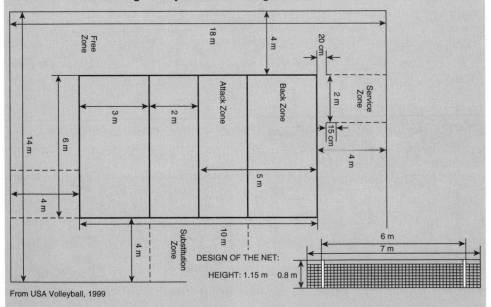

From USA Volleyball, 1999

been included in the Paralympic Games. By 1984, international competition was developed to include those players with arm and leg disabilities as well as those with amputations. In 2000, both Sitting and Standing National Championships were infused into the United States Volleyball National Championships.

SUMMARY

- The game of volleyball requires cooperation and communication. A team consists of six players on the court, arranged in a rotational order. The serving team plays defense first, then transitions to offense, then back to defense, and so on, until the rally is ended. Traditionally, points are scored when the receiving team does not successfully return the ball. In rally scoring, each rally wins a point whether it is won by the serving or receiving team.
- During play, attackers have the options of spiking the ball across the court, down the line, tipping the ball over the block, or hitting an off-speed shot into the opponents' court. The attacker may hit the ball from the option side of the court or hit from the power side.
- Volleyball is a game of rebound and movement. The size of the court is relatively small for the number of players, creating a congested area. The game has evolved into one of efficiency, accuracy, and supportive movements. Each team has a maximum of three contacts with which to accomplish the game's objective, to return the ball and have it contact the floor on the opponents' side of the net within the boundaries of their court.
- Apparel for volleyball include appropriate shoes. They are extremely lightweight with added cushioning in the inner and outer soles. The sole is flat with good ankle, arch, and heel supports. Knee pads are an optional part of the volleyball uniform for indoor play. It is recommended that knee protection be worn, particularly while learning. Uniforms range from long sleeve to sleeveless tops and form-fitting shorts.
- William G. Morgan, physical director of the Holyoke, Massachusetts, YMCA, created a game for men called Mintonette in 1895, which rapidly evolved to volleyball in 1896. The game spread rapidly throughout the world as a result of YMCA missionaries in the early 1900s in Canada, Central and South America, and Southeast Asia. During World War I, the game was furthered in Europe. After World War I, volleyball experienced a huge growth in the United States. The first interscholastic program, the first collegiate intramural program, and the first AAU national activity were conducted in the early 1920s. World War II furthered the worldwide participation in the game. Soon after the war, intercollegiate volleyball for women began to gain popularity as did USVBA involvement. In the 1964 Olympic Games, men's and women's volleyball was added to provide permanent international visibility for the game. The United States, by the end of the 1980s, had established itself as a world volleyball power. By the 1990s, volleyball had become the second most popular sport played in the United States. In the 1990s, professional men's and women's teams began to surface worldwide.

- Volleyball is played extensively by those who benefit directly through participation. The development of Special Olympics Unified Volleyball, sitting volleyball, and standing volleyball make the game a sport for all.

▶ **rotational order (serving order)   p. 2**
i.e., right back (1), right front (2), middle front (3), left front (4), left back (5), and middle back (6)

▶ **spikers (hitters, attackers)   p. 2**
players who attack the ball with a downward direction, generally from the front court

▶ **blockers   p. 2**
players, located in the front court, who block the ball

▶ **backs   p. 2**
players who serve as passers and defense in the back court

▶ **overlap   p. 3**
a rule, based on foot placement, when the ball is served

▶ **points   p. 3**
the method of keeping score; one point is scored per designated result according to rules

▶ **sideout   p. 3**
When the serving team loses the ball after a rally, the receiving team gets the ball. This is called a sideout.

▶ **rally scoring   p. 3**
a point is scored when either team wins the rally

▶ **setter   p. 3**
the player who is designated to organize and execute the team's offensive play

▶ **switch   p. 3**
During the serve, players on the court may exchange positions, thereby moving into positions that best suit the offensive dynamics of their team.

▶ **setting options   p. 3**
offensive plays used by the setter to facilitate the team's offensive play

▶ **dig   p. 3**
using a forearm pass fist, or top of a hand, to play a ball that is in a low movement zone as a result of a hard hit attack

▶ **forearm pass   p. 3**
Any ball arriving at or below the player's waist can be easily passed using the forearms as the contacting surface.

▶ **emergency techniques   p. 3**
a method of retrieving a ball that is outside the player's range of effectiveness

▶ **spike   p. 3**
the attempt by the offensive team to end play by hitting the ball to the floor of the defensive team

▶ **crosscourt/down-the-line/dinking (tipping)/off-speed attacks   p. 3**
attacks generated from a variety of areas on the court and directed to specific areas of the opposite court

▶ **option/off-hand side of the court   p. 3**
the right side of your team's court when the attacker is right-handed

▶ **power side of the court   p. 3**
the left side of the court when the attacker is right-handed

▶ **offensive/defensive systems   p. 3**
organized plays used by either the attacking team or the defending team

▶ **multiple offensive system** p. 3
a playing system that uses a setter from the back court, thereby allowing 3 attackers in the front court, e.g., 6-2; 5-1

▶ **traditional offensive system** p. 3
a playing system that uses two attackers and one setter in the front court, i.e., 4-2

▶ **player-back defense** p. 3
one player drops back to the endline while the two side players move to their respective sidelines

▶ **Libero** p. 3
a defensive specialist who may substitute for any back court player

▶ **zones of movement** p. 4
low, medium, high, or airborne movement of the body

▶ **technique** p. 5
how the ball is played

▶ **FIVB** p. 5
Federation Internationale de Volleyball, the international governing body of volleyball

▶ **NCAA** p. 6
National Collegiate Athletic Association

▶ **USVBA/USA Volleyball** p. 7
United States Volleyball Association, also known as USA Volleyball; the national governing body of volleyball

▶ **DGWS** p. 7
(Division for Girls' and Women's Sports) forerunner to the National Association for Girls and Women in Sport, responsible for writing and administering the

rules of the women's collegiate game in the United States

▶ **AIAW** p. 10
Association of Intercollegiate Athletics for Women, initially responsible for the administration of intercollegiate women's volleyball championships in the United States

▶ **NAGWS** p. 10
National Association for Girls and Women in Sport, responsible for writing the rules of the women's collegiate game in the United States

▶ **NFSHSA** p. 10
National Federation of State High School Associations, responsible for writing the rules of the high school game in the United States

▶ **swing offense** p. 11
an offensive system used by the USA men's team which was based upon an attack from the inside working out

▶ **Special Olympics Unified Volleyball** p. 13
teams which include Special Olympians and partners with rule modifications; part of Special Olympics International

▶ **sitting volleyball** p. 13
teams of players who play from a seated position with rule modifications; part of Disabled Sports

▶ **standing volleyball** p. 13
teams composed by a specified number of points resulting from appendage loss; part of Disabled Sports

Assessment 1-1

Directions: Read each question carefully. Select the **most** appropriate answer.

1. Which best describes the basic ready position as the player anticipates the arrival of the ball during serve reception?
   a. feet slightly narrower apart than shoulders; weight toward the outside of the feet
   b. feet slightly wider apart than shoulders; weight distributed on inside balls of the feet
   c. feet slightly narrower apart than shoulders; weight on inside balls of the feet
   d. feet slightly wider apart than shoulders; weight toward the outside of the feet

2. By its nature, the game of volleyball requires
   a. hustle and drive.
   b. cooperation and communication.
   c. arrogance and persistence.
   d. patience and perseverance.

3. Most American sports are games of _____. The game of volleyball is a game of _____ and _____.
   a. rebound; movement; jumping
   b. possession; cooperation; diving
   c. rebound; movement; diving
   d. possession; rebound; movement

4. Who was the originator of volleyball and in what year did it begin?
   a. William Morgan; 1895
   b. William Neville; 1905
   c. Taras Liskevych; 1892
   d. YMCA; 1900

5. Which country introduced volleyball as a modern Olympic sport?
   a. Cuba
   b. Soviet Union
   c. United States
   d. Japan

6. The members of a volleyball officiating team include the following:
   a. first referee; second referee; coach; players
   b. first referee; second referee; scorekeeper; two or four line judges
   c. first referee; second referee; coach; players; scorekeeper
   d. first referee; second referee; coach; players; scorekeeper; two or four line judges

7. Two key points in the dive and catch include the following:
   a. reach out with both arms in front of the body; transfer weight onto the ball of the forward foot
   b. reach out with one arm to the side of the body; transfer weight onto the ball of the forward foot
   c. reach out with both arms in front of the body; transfer weight onto the knee of the forward leg
   d. reach out with both arms to the side of the body; transfer weight onto the knee of the forward leg
8. The basic body movement zones in the game of volleyball are
   a. supportive and lateral movement.
   b. backward and forward movement.
   c. lateral, medium, and low movement.
   d. airborne, high, medium, and low movement.
9. The serve is the skill used to put the ball into play. The types of serves include the following:
   a. underhand floater; overhand floater; overhand topspin
   b. underhand backspin; overhand topspin
   c. jump; sidearm; underhand backspin
   d. underhand floater; sidearm; overhand topspin
10. During three-player attack coverage, what pattern is formed by the players around the attacker?
    a. a star pattern
    b. a "V" pattern
    c. a "W" pattern
    d. a cup pattern

True/False

Directions: Write a + for **True,** write a **0** if any portion of the statement is **False.**

1. The low movement zone is the most frequently used zone in the game of volleyball.
2. Eye movements are considered basic in volleyball play.
3. The larger the area of visual concentration, the less chance for error when the ball is contacted.
4. The overhead pass is the key to the beginning of any team's offensive system.
5. Primary points of contact on the ball during overhead passing are those that supply power.
6. The primary objective of the block is to become the only line of defense and seal off the net.
7. During overlapping, the players' shoulders are used to determine if a violation has occurred.

8. The winning team serves first at the beginning of the second game of the match.
9. Using the head to hit the ball may be considered legal in volleyball play.
10. Two major objectives in the process of becoming an official are to develop an understanding of the game and to gain practical experience.
11. A down the line serve usually sets up a crosscourt pass.
12. The serve can be considered the initial defensive technique employed by a team.
13. Drifting moves the body vertically rather than laterally at takeoff on a spike.
14. When single blocking on sets close to the net, the ball should be roofed.
15. The 5–1 offensive system utilizes the primary setter from the back court only.

Short Answer

Directions: Write complete answers that answer each question specifically.

1. Why should the feet be in a front-to-back position during the performance of an overhead pass? During setting, does it matter which foot is forward when the ball is less than three feet from the net? If yes, why? If no, why not?
2. Who determines if an overhead pass is performed legally during a game?
3. In what specific situations is a forearm pass used during play?
4. What is a dink?
5. Which skill in volleyball uses the "Mickey Mouse Ears" ready position? Why?
6. What is the basic difference between performance of the overhand floater serve and the overhand topspin serve?
7. What was the original purpose of the jump serve during a game?
8. What are two important factors when anticipating digging a ball from a hard-driven attack?
9. What is one strength of a player-up defense? What is one strength of a player-back defense?
10. What are the four basic zones of movement used by each player in volleyball?
11. In what country was the game of volleyball invented? By whom was it invented?
12. What organization is credited for spreading volleyball internationally during the early 1900s? Why?
13. What organization controls and regulates the amateur sport of volleyball internationally today? What events led up to this?
14. What does the term "balancing the court" mean? When should it be used in a game?
15. What are two key points necessary to remember when performing a back overhead pass?

Answers to
Assessment 1-1

Multiple Choice Answers

1. b
2. b
3. d
4. a
5. d

6. b
7. a
8. d
9. a
10. d

True/False Answers

1. 0
2. +
3. 0
4. 0
5. +
6. 0
7. 0
8. 0

9. +
10. +
11. +
12. +
13. 0
14. +
15. 0

Short Answer

1. For improved front-to-back balance. Yes, it matters. The right foot should be in front of the left to avoid setting the ball over the net.
2. The first referee.
3. It is the team's first contact and assists in reducing the speed of the ball when passing to the setter. It can also be used to dig a high-speed attack.
4. Using an off-speed movement initially resembling an attack to contact the ball to place it just over or around the block.
5. The block.
6. The follow-through action is stopped during the performance of the overhand floater serve.
7. It was originally developed for the men's game. The height of the men's net in volleyball creates a different trajectory with most traditional serves.
8. The speed of the oncoming ball and the speed of the player's reaction time.
9. Player-up: If the contact of the attack has created a lofted arc on the ball, the short area of the court must be covered. Player-back: When the speed of the

ball is rapid, but the ball has been lofted over the block or between the block, the deep area of the court must be covered.

10. Airborne; high; medium; low.
11. United States; William Morgan.
12. Young Men's Christian Association (YMCA).
13. International Volleyball Federation (FIVB).
14. Responsibilities for critical zones of the court must be given during each play, depending upon team court coverage. The court is balanced by dividing the zone between players by size of available space and according to the weakness within the zone.
15. Movement prior to contact should be identical to the front pass; at ball contact, hips are thrust forward quickly.

Assessment 1-2 You Make the Call

Through the use of photos, a brief overview of the necessities of the game, playing systems of the game, and physical preparation for the game can be achieved. By studying the photos and answering the questions below each photo, your visual skills can be sharpened. This is one way of learning how to recognize efficient movement and good mechanics. The answers are located at the end of this chapter.

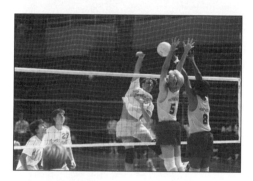

FIGURE 1-6 Are the offensive players effectively supporting the attacker in the attack coverage? Courtesy of Jenny Walsh/USAV.

FIGURE 1-7 Was the timing of the double block attempt effective enough for both players to contribute to the block? Courtesy of the University of Central Oklahoma Photographic Services.

FIGURE 1-8 Was the double block effectively set? Courtesy of Jenny Walsh/USAV.

FIGURE 1-9 Are the kneepads of this player appropriately positioned? Courtesy of D. Kluka.

FIGURE 1-10 Does the player form a "window" for executing an overhead pass? Courtesy of D. Kluka.

FIGURE 1-11 Did the passer actually see the ball contact her arms? Courtesy of Michael Hood.

FIGURE 1-12 Are the arms and hands appropriately positioned for an efficient pass? Courtesy of Clint Carlton.

FIGURE 1-13 Are the arms and hands most efficiently placed for an over-head pass? Courtesy of Clint Carlton.

FIGURE 1-14 Is this an efficient follow-through for an overhead floater serve? Courtesy of Clint Carlton.

FIGURE 1-15 Did the attacker use a high seam? Courtesy of Rafael "Boy" Inocentes Philippine Sports Commission.

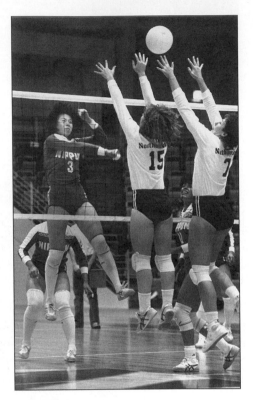

FIGURE 1-16 Will the attacker be successful in placing the ball around the blocker's hands? Courtesy of Northwestern University Sports Information.

FIGURE 1-17 Has Blocker #7 drifted? Courtesy of Northwestern Sports Information.

Photo Answers—Assessment 1-2

Figure 1-6

NO. The players should have been positioned in a low movement zone, anticipating the rebound of the blocked ball.

Figure 1-7

YES.

Figure 1-8

NO. The middle blocker did not close to the outside blocker in order to complete the double block attempt.

Figure 1-9

YES.

Figure 1-10

YES.

Figure 1-11

NO. She should have focused tightly on the ball as it contacted her arms.

Figure 1-12

YES. Notice that the thumbs are directed toward the floor and forearms are flat for an even platform.

Figure 1-13

NO. The hands should be higher so that the thumbs are near the eyebrows.

Figure 1-14

YES. The follow-through action is stopped as contact is made.

Figure 1-15

YES. The ball was attacked between the hands of the two blockers.

Figure 1-16

YES. The blocker has reached the height of her jump.

Figure 1-17

YES. Notice that most of her weight is toward the left. She also had to drift to the left to reach to the ball.

CHAPTER 2

FACILITIES AND **EQUIPMENT: VITAL** TO THE GAME

OBJECTIVES

After reading this chapter, you should be able to do the following:

- Have a basic understanding of a volleyball court and its playing area.
- Describe the basic equipment needed to play the indoor and beach games.

KEY TERMS

While reading this chapter, you will become familiar with the following terms:

▶ playing area

▶ sidelines

▶ endlines

▶ attack lines

▶ front zone

▶ back zone

▶ service zone

▶ substitution zone

▶ warmup area

▶ scoreboard

▶ side bands

Volleyball is one of the most inexpensive sports to establish facilities and equipment for. The indoor game requires only a court, net, posts, antennae, and a ball to begin. For the beach game, sand, net, posts, rope, and a ball are all that are needed.

THE INDOOR GAME

THE PLAYING AREA

The **playing area** includes the court (front and back zones), other designated areas surrounding the court (free, substitution, and serving zones), and the space above these areas. All lines on the court are 5 cm (2″) wide and must be of colors which contrast with the playing court and any other lines imposed on the court. Two **sidelines** and two **endlines** comprise the court boundaries. These lines are considered part of the court. A center line divides the court into two equal parts and extends from one sideline to the other. **Attack lines** are located 3 m (9′ 10″) from the center line. The court measures 59′ 6″ from the outside edge of each end-line and 29′ 6″ from the outside edge of the sidelines

The **front zone** consists of an area that is delimited by the center line and the attack line. This area extends beyond the sidelines. The **back zone** consists of an area delimited by the attack line and endline. The area extends beyond the side-lines as well. The **service zone** is 9 m (29′ 6″) wide and is located behind and excluding each end line. It should have a minimum depth of 2 m (6′ 6″) so that servers can feel comfortable in the space provided. The **substitution zone** is an imaginary extension of the two attack lines, including the scorekeeper's table. The **warmup area** is 3 m × 3 m (9′ 10″ × 9′ 10″) and is located even with each team bench.

SCOREBOARD

A **scoreboard** should be provided. It should be divided into two parts with sufficient numbers to display each team's score (generally up to thirty points per team). Although the score displayed is not official, it facilitates each game for players, coaches, and spectators.

SIDE BANDS

Two **side bands**, 5 cm (2″) wide, of white are vertically attached to the net, in line with, and perpendicular to, each sideline. They are part of the net.

ANTENNAE

An **antenna** is a red and white striped rod which is flexible, 1.8 m (5′) long and 10 mm in diameter. Generally made of fiberglass, it is attached to the outer side of each side band of the net. The top of each antenna should be 80 cm (32″) above the height of the net. The antennae are considered part of the net.

NET

The **net** is 1 m (39″) in width and at least 9.5 m (32′) long. It divides the playing area into two equal courts by being strung across the court from sideline to sideline. The top and the bottom must be attached to two posts, both located outside the court. It must be constructed of black square mesh with a white band across the top, 5 cm (2″) wide. The height of the net is 2.43 m (7′ 11″) for men and 2.24 m (7′ $4\frac{1}{8}$″) for women. The net height is measured at the center line in the center of the court.

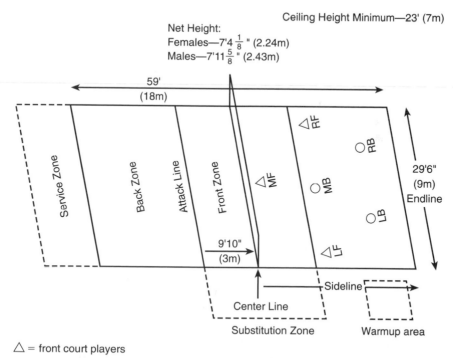

$\triangle$ = front court players

$\bigcirc$ = back court players

FIGURE 2-1 Court dimensions and player positions.

BALL

The spherical ball must be made of leather with a rubber or rubber-like bladder. It is light in color with a maximum of no more than 25 percent of its exterior covered by print. It should weigh between 260 to 280 g (9 to 10 oz) and have a circumference of between 65 to 67 cm ($25\frac{1}{2}''$ to $27''$). Ball pressure should range between 0.30 to 0.325 kg/cm (4.3 to 4.6 lb/sq in).

FIGURE 2-2 Official volleyball; 18 panels.

WEARING APPAREL THAT IS FORBIDDEN

Jewelry is not allowed. Religious or medical medallions and flat-band wedding rings, however, can be worn as long as they are removed from chains and taped to or sewn under the uniform. Braces, casts, or head ornamentation cannot be worn if it could be determined that players could gain tactical advantage.

THE BEACH GAME

Beach volleyball was established as an Olympic medal sport at the 1996 Summer Games in Atlanta, Georgia, with twenty-four men's teams and eighteen women's teams. The team of Karch Kiraly/Kent Steffes dominated the men's pro tour in the 1990s and became the first gold medalists in 1996. Over the past thirty years there has been a rapid growth of the game, particularly in the United States and Brazil. Presently, the beach game requires the overall development of players. It has been determined that, in the men's international game, rallies last around twenty seconds. Jumps are executed, on average, every forty-two seconds. There are also eighty-five jumps per player per hour of play, and 234 running starts are performed per game. The running starts occur approximately once every fifteen seconds. During a weekend tournament, players participate in a minimum of seven and a maximum of ten matches. With this as a backdrop for the present-day beach requirements, the game's development has been interesting.

Beach volleyball was initially played in the 1920s in Santa Monica, California, USA. Rules were originally adapted from the 6-on-6 indoor rules of the times. By the 1930s, the game was played with teams of four. By the late 1930s, teams were composed of two players. To escape the Great Depression, people went to the beach and played volleyball.

Prior to the 1940s, spiking and blocking were not permitted. The net was also lower than its height today. Because of the draft for World War II, young American men drifted away from the beach game. Play during 1941 through 1945 was almost nonexistent. After the war, beach volleyball was resurrected, and the first tournament was played in 1947 at State Beach, Santa Monica, California.

As early as 1951, those responsible for the tournaments were interested in developing the beach game as a spectator sport. Because spiking and blocking were not a part of the beach game, matches lasted several hours. To facilitate spectators, organizers included beauty contests during the tournaments. This addition prompted media and spectator attention. The beach game was soon viewed as a social event as well as an athletic one. Beach volleyball meccas were established at State and Sorrento Beaches in Santa Monica, Marine Street in Manhattan Beach, and East Beach in Santa Barbara, all in Southern California.

By the early 1950s, the spike and block were also introduced to the game. This addition prompted the opportunity for the development of superstars, whose stellar spiking performances and two-person team thinking encouraged individual notoriety. Gene Selznick was beach volleyball's first superstar. He was a legendary indoor and beach player in the 1950s and early 1960s. During the 1960s, the superstar notoriety, coupled with the beach, sun, sand, and parties, established a perception of beach volleyball as a game for those who wanted to live the shorts, tank tops, sunglasses, and relaxed lifestyle.

In the mid-1960s, Ron von Hagen popularized the bump set for service reception. One of the most successful players of all-time, he established a record of sixty-two open victories and retired in 1978. In 1965, the California Beach Volleyball Association was founded. Tournament organizers coordinated schedules and defined the rules of the game.

Prior to 1976, prize money for beach play was negligible. Although players trained for several hours a day, financial support for players was unavailable. The first World Championships in 1976 were held at the State Beach in Santa Monica. The winners of this event, Jim Menges/Greg Lee, earned $5000 in prize money. More than 30,000 spectators attended the event. The combination of excellent game play and huge spectator numbers prompted a marketing agency, Event Concepts, to promote and expand the beach tour. Chris Marlowe, noted television analyst of volleyball in the 1990s, and Jim Menges won the World Championships at State Beach in 1977. Jose Cuervo was the first major sponsor of the beach game in 1978. By 1983, professional tournaments had expanded to twelve. Total prize money increased to $137,000, sponsored by Jose Cuervo and Miller Beer. Those promoting the tournament implemented a variety of rule changes as well as substantial portions of television and sponsor money. With unrest building between the marketing agency and the players, players protested and asked for an increase in prize money available to them. When those in control refused, the players formed the Association of Volleyball Professionals (AVP). The players expected to improve their position within the administration of the league. Unfortunately, the demand for more rights and knowledge of league financial status as well as the formation of the AVP proved insufficient. The only alternative was a player strike. The World Championship in 1984 at Redondo Beach, California, was played without the best players in beach volleyball. Sponsors of the event, concerned about the quality of play, decided to negotiate with the AVP. The AVP had been successful in securing the power position for beach volleyball promotion. Bolle Sunglasses joined as a major sponsor.

The tournament series increased to fourteen, and total prize money blossomed to $275,000.

Beach volleyball made its network television debut in 1986 on ABC's *Wide World of Sports,* and cable television exposure through *Prime Ticket* provided substantive exposure for further promotion of the game. Those players who dominated play in the mid-1980s for a decade included Sinjin Smith, Karch Kiraly, Mike Dodd, Tim Hovland, and Randy Stoklos. In 1989, Sinjin Smith/Randy Stoklos won more than 100 tournament titles, becoming the most successful beach volleyball team in the history of the game. Tournament prize money had increased to $1,700,000.

Interestingly, the FIVB held its first men's beach volleyball World Championships in 1987. Prize money from 1987 to 1990 totalled $493,340 with eleven events during the three years. By the 1998 season, there were sixteen events, with prize money at $2,490,000.

In 1992, Karch Kiraly/Kent Steffes won thirteen consecutive tournaments, tying the record set by Jim Menges/Greg Lee in 1976–1977. By 1993, more than 500,000 spectators watched beach tournaments, and prize money exploded to $3,700,000. Multimillion dollar contracts with Jose Cuervo, Miller, Old Spice, and Coca Cola had been signed. The 1995 and 1996 AVP tours offered twenty-seven and twenty-four events, respectively, with prize money at $4,500,000.

Escalating costs, including a decline in spectator attendance, television contracts, and increasing prize money demands, placed the AVP in a financially vulnerable situation. After the 1998 season, the AVP, established only fifteen years before, filed for bankruptcy. The organization, comprised of the world's best beach volleyball players, whose goal was to maximize the game while protecting the commercial interests and integrity of its players, had to restructure.

In the women's beach game, Jean Brunicardi established prominence in the 1960s. The most successful players before the formation of the professional volleyball association for women included Kathy Gregory in the 1970s, and Nina Matthies and Jackie Silva in the 1980s. Matthies was instrumental in the 1987 formation of the Women's Pro Volleyball Association (WPVA). The establishment of a separate women's league was to professionalize the women's game in its own right, and to administer, govern, and protect the integrity of the women's game. Prior to 1987, prize money was negligible.

By 1988, sponsors expanded prize money from $50,000 to $100,000. WPVA tournaments were placed on television. By 1991, prize money increased to $665,000, and the number of tournaments was expanded to seventeen. In 1993, however, events were reduced to fourteen, and prize money fell to $352,000. Spectator attendance in just two years began to diminish, a television contract was lost, an increase took place in organizing costs, prize money was diminished by twenty percent, and the overall schedule was decreased to twelve.

With a roller coaster financial basis, eight top players defected to a newly established AVP women's tour in 1993. Although the AVP presented potentially a more lucrative opportunity for players, the AVP had difficulty providing a meaningful women's tour. As a result, the top women players returned to the WPVA in 1994. Fifteen events, $639,000 in prize money, and an enormous financial undertaking was put forward by the owners of the league. After the disappointing performance of the women's indoor team at the 1996 Olympic Games in Atlanta (eighth place), the WPVA struggled with attendance and sponsorship. In April, 1998, the owners of the WPVA were forced to dissolve the organization. WPVA stars in the 1990s included Patty Dodd, Nancy Reno, Holley McPeak, Karolyn Kirby, and Liz Masakayan.

Contrastingly, the FIVB initiated its first women's event in 1992, to encourage the development of beach volleyball in anticipation of the 1996 Olympic Games and beach's premiere as an Olympic medal sport. In 1993, the first FIVB women's World Championships were initiated. At its beginning in 1992, only two events were held, with prize money totalling $100,000. By 1998, nine events were held with prize money rising to $1,550,000.

The evolution of beach volleyball internationally is still in its infancy. Much depends upon the development of players who begin at early ages. Historically, elite players' average ages were in the mid-thirties. Typically, they have played the beach game after they completed successful indoor careers. The FIVB, as a result of the Olympic Games in 1996, promised the creation of an international training center for beach volleyball just outside Atlanta, Georgia. Presently, little has been done to develop this legacy promised to those in the United States. Its purpose is to develop the beach game for players and coaches throughout the world. It remains to be seen what effect an international training center for beach volleyball might have on the worldwide development of the beach game.

BEACH TIMELINE

- 1948—first two-man beach tournament held at State Beach in Santa Monica, CA
- 1950s—open tournaments held at 5 California beaches: Santa Barbara, State, Corona del Mar, Laguna Beach, and San Diego
- 1960—First Manhattan Beach Open. It was the oldest and most prestigious event on the men's pro beach tour.
- 1976—first significant pro tournament, won by Menges/Lee
- 1977—Ron von Hagen retires with 62 tournament victories.
- 1979—Kiraly/Smith won 5 tournaments.
- 1980—Kiraly/Smith won 5 tournaments.
- 1983—AVP tour is formed
- 1986—Beach volleyball debuts on ABC's *Wide World of Sports.*
- 1987—Women's Pro Volleyball Association formed
- 1988—AVP signs 3-year contract with Miller Brewing. Prize money reaches $1.5 M/year.
- 1989—Smith first player to win 100 tournaments
- 1993—NBC broadcasts 10 AVP events. Prize money is $3.7 M/year.
- 1993—IOC votes to include beach volleyball in the Olympic Games.
- 1996—Prize money on the AVP tour is $4.5 M/year.

- 1996—Beach volleyball debuts in the Olympic Games.
- 1998—AVP files for bankruptcy.
- 1998—WPVA is dissolved.
- 2000—Olympic Games in Sydney, Australia

THE PLAYING AREA

Court dimensions and the surrounding free zone are the same as in the indoor game. The playing area surface, however, must consist of fine-grained sand that should be at least 30 cm (12″) deep. The lines on the court consist of two sidelines and two endlines, as well as a center line, all of which should be in contrasting colors to the sand's playing surface.

NET AND POSTS

The net and posts should be the same as those used in the indoor game. The top band, however, should be made from navy or bright, colored canvas for improved visibility. The height of the net should be 2.43 m ($7'11\frac{5}{8}''$) for men and 2.24 m ($7'4\frac{1}{8}''$) for women. The posts must be 30 cm to 1 m (12″ to 39″) outside each of the sidelines and free from sharp edges, just as in the indoor game.

ANTENNAE AND SIDE BANDS

These are optional equipment and will be determined by those who host the tournament and the regulations of each tournament.

BALL

The spherical ball can be made of leather or water-resistant material. The inside bladder is made of rubber or a derivative of rubber. It will be 65 cm to 67 cm ($25\frac{1}{2}''$ to $26\frac{1}{2}''$) in circumference and weigh 260 g (9 oz) to 280 g (10 oz). The ball can be one solid color or multicolored. Ball pressure should be between 0.175 to 0.225 kg/cm (2.5 to 3.2 lb/sq in).

SUMMARY

- Playing area for the indoor game includes the court (front and back zones), other designated areas surrounding the court (free, substitution, and serving zones), and the space above these areas. Sidelines, endlines, and attack lines comprise lineage of the area. A scoreboard, net, antennae, side bands, and ball complete the equipment needed for play.

- The beach game has slightly different facilities, equipment, and history. The playing surface must consist of fine-grained sand that should be at least 30 cm (12″) deep. Net color differs from the indoor game, and antennae and side bands are optional.

- Beach volleyball was established as an Olympic medal sport at the 1996 Summer Games in Atlanta. It was initially begun, however, in the 1920s in Santa Monica, California, USA. Because the beach game generally involves teams of two, the game became a "natural" for the promotion of "star" athletes.

- The evolution of beach volleyball internationally is still in its infancy. Much depends upon the development of players who begin at early ages. It remains to be seen what effect an international training center for beach volleyball might have on the worldwide development of the beach game.

▶ **playing area   p. 32**
the front and back zones of the court, the free, substitution, and serving zones

▶ **sidelines   p. 32**
boundaries of the court on either side

▶ **endlines   p. 32**
boundaries of the court on either end

▶ **attack lines   p. 32**
boundaries of the court which delineate from where a back row attack can be generated

▶ **front zone   p. 32**
playing area that is delimited by the center line and the attack line

▶ **back zone   p. 32**
playing area that is delimited by the attack line and endline

▶ **service zone   p. 32**
playing area located behind each endline

▶ **substitution zone   p. 32**
playing area that is an imaginary extension of the attack lines, including the scorekeeper's table

▶ **warmup area   p. 32**
playing area located even with the bench

▶ **scoreboard   p. 32**
a visible scorekeeping device for teams throughout the match, generally divided into two parts, with sufficient numbers to display each team's score

▶ **side bands   p. 32**
vertical bands, attached to the net, in line with and perpendicular to each sideline

CHAPTER 3

RULES AND
TERMINOLOGY
OF THE GAME

OBJECTIVES

After reading this chapter, you should be able to do the following:

- Explain the basic rules of the indoor and beach games.
- Have a complete understanding of how to play the basic game of volleyball.
- Understand the basic language used in volleyball.
- Know how to analyze a match.

KEY TERMS

While reading this chapter, you will become familiar with the following terms:

- ► prematch protocol
- ► Rally Point Scoring
- ► ball contact
- ► play between the attack lines
- ► officiating team
- ► basic skills of the game
- ► fundamental terminology

The game of volleyball is one of the most exciting and dynamic games in the world. Its rules are constantly evolving to become better suited for spectators.

The Federation Internationale de Volleyball (FIVB) is the international governing body for volleyball in the world. Its rules are used by many countries and during international competition. Sources for detailed volleyball rules include the following:

High School Rules:
National Federation of State High School Associations (NFSHSA)
11724 Plaza Circle
Kansas City, MO 64195

Collegiate Rules—women:
National Association for Girls and Women in Sports (NAGWS)
1900 Association Drive
Reston, VA 20191

All others:
USA Volleyball (USAV)
715 South Circle Drive
Colorado Springs, CO 80910-2368

PRE-MATCH PROTOCOL

Before a match, both teams warm up by rehearsing skills through drillwork. They share the entire playing area with the other team while stretching and jogging. They also perform serving and ball handling drills. Generally, the serving team takes possession of the court first, followed by the other team for the same designated amount of time, and both share the court for a designated time period. After the introduction of the teams and coaches, the teams meet at center court and exchange small gifts and handshakes under the net. The match begins immediately thereafter.

Generally, the following format could be used prior to a match. The ultimate decision, however, is based upon the host team, tournament, or conference regulations. One hour prior to beginning the match, for one-half hour the court is available to both teams for warmup. The thirty minutes prior to the start of the match is broken down to focus on these points:

- First ten minutes—shared use of court by both teams
- Next five minutes—serving team on full court (team to serve first in the match)
- Next five minutes—receiving team on full court
- Next two minutes—both teams warm up with serving
- International Teams march in
- National anthem, officials and teams introductions
- First serve

FIGURE 3-1 Pre-match discussion. Courtesy of D. Kluka.

FIGURE 3-2 Preparing prior to the first serve. Courtesy of D. Kluka.

SCORING POINTS, PLAYERS, SUBSTITUTIONS

The team winning the coin toss before the match has the option of serving or receiving first or choice of side of the court. The team serving first in game 1 also serves first in game 3; the team then receives first in games 2 and 4. If game 5 is necessary, another coin toss determines the serving team.

Volleyball is a dynamic sport. Those in charge of the rules have attempted to balance offensive and defensive play in order to make the sport more interesting and marketable for television.

In October, 1998, the FIVB Congress meeting in Tokyo adopted the Rally Point Scoring system. It became effective on January 1, 2000.

In **Rally Point Scoring,** each rally wins a point whether it is won by the serving or receiving team. The revised rules also provide that matches are played for the best of five games (set). The first four games are played to twenty-five points. The fifth game, if necessary, is played to fifteen points. A team must win a game by two points.

A player must initiate service within eight seconds of the first referee's whistle that indicates service.

Prior to each serve, players must be in the correct serving rotational order in relation to their teammates. Once the ball is contacted for the serve, players may switch to anywhere on the court. However, based on their service rotational order, back court players may not block. Back court players may not attack the ball while on or in front of the 3 m attack line. They may, however, attack if their takeoff for the attack begins behind the 3 m attack line.

Overlapping of positions cannot occur at the moment of service. Overlapping is determined by the position of players' feet.

A team is permitted six substitutions per game. When a player is replaced by another, he or she must reenter for the same player in the same position. (NAGWS modification permits an unlimited number of individual entries within the allowed 15 total team substitutions; beginning the game counts as one entry. The NAGWS rule also permits more than two players to substitute in the same position. For example, A starts the game; B substitutes for A; C substitutes for B; A substitutes for C.)

BALL CONTACT

Brief contact with the ball must occur. If the ball comes to rest momentarily in the hands or on the arms, an illegal hit has taken place.

A player may legitimately use any part of the body to play the ball.

PLAY BETWEEN THE ATTACK LINES

Players may not touch the net while playing the ball. If the player has insignificant contact with the net, it is not a fault. Players may not cross the center line completely. A player may, however, touch the opponent's court with hands or feet provided some part of the penetrating hands or feet remain either in contact with or directly above the center line. Contact with any other part of the body (except hair) is a fault.

Reaching across the net is permitted during the follow-through of an attack or when the offensive team has completed its attack and the defense is blocking. Players may not interfere into the opponent's opportunity to play the ball.

FIGURE 3.3 An overhead pass. Brief contact with the ball must occur. Courtesy of Michael F. Hood.

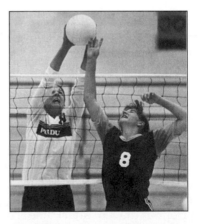

FIGURE 3.4 A single block. Courtesy of Purdue University Photographic Center for Instructional Services.

The block does not count as a contact; therefore, a team blocking the ball has three additional contacts if desired. The blocker is permitted a second consecutive contact of the ball immediately thereafter.

The ball must pass over the net completely between the two antennae or their imaginary extensions, which are located directly above the vertical tape markers on the net at the sidelines.

TIME

Usually there is no designated game time limit. A match (three of five games) may last from forty-five minutes to three hours.

Time between each game is three minutes.

Time outs for substitutions must occur efficiently and without delay.

Each team is permitted two time outs per game. The length of a time out will be governed by the rule under which the game is being played (e.g., thirty seconds, forty-five seconds, one minute, or one minute fifteen seconds).

OFFICIATING TEAM

The officiating team is composed of a first or "up" referee and a second or "down" referee. The first referee stands on a platform that is opposite the team benches. The first referee is responsible for controlling the match and focusing on the handling of the ball. The second referee stands on the floor on the opposite side of the court from the first referee. This official is responsible for the net, center line violations, and substitutions. If there is a difference of opinion between any of the officials, the first referee has the final decision.

Two or four line judges are used to assist in the determination of whether a ball is in or out of bounds and whether a ball was touched by a player. The first referee has the authority to accept or reject the call made by the line judge as well.

To round out the officiating team, an official scorekeeper is positioned at the officials' table, seated directly opposite the first referee. This official is responsible for recording the exact details of the match according to official symbols used in volleyball scorebooks. For specific details on officiating, see Appendix A.

THE BASIC SKILLS OF THE GAME

A brief summary of the skills involved in playing the game of volleyball will help to set the stage for chapters 5, 6, and 7. Understanding these skills is most important for success.

- The serve: the way in which the game is begun and the ball is put into play after a rally. A floater, topspin, or jump serve is frequently used.

FIGURE 3.5A & B Effective uses of timeouts. Courtesy of D. Kluka.

FIGURE 3.6 Approaching a joust. Courtesy of Rafael "Boy" Inocentes Philippine Sports Commission.

- The forearm pass: generally the first contact of the ball after the serve. This allows for the passer to direct the ball to an area of the court designated for the setter.
- The set: the skill used as the primary link to initiate a team's offensive system. The setter contacts the ball using both hands simultaneously, directs the offense, and decides which attacker gets set. Some teams use two designated setters; others use one. A set may be a front set, a back set, a jump set, or a setter attack. By having a variety of setting options available, blocking becomes quite difficult.

- The attack: the most explosive skill used in the game. The attack can be used to generate speed and force on the ball, to hit the ball where the opponents cannot get to it, to hit around the block, to tip or dink over the block, or to use the block to win the rally.
- The block: used as the first line of defense. The block can be used to immediately win the rally or at least slow down the ball so the ball can be converted into an offensive play. Single, double, and triple blocks can be used to seal off portions of the net to the attackers.
- The dig: usually used when the ball is hit from a full speed attack. A defensive player must get to the ball so the setter has an opportunity to convert the ball to an offensive play. The body is always in a low position when digging. The digger may already be in a low position, perfectly anticipating the attacker's hit; emergency techniques such as dives and rolls may also be used.

VOLLEYBALL TERMINOLOGY

Many volleyball terms are familiar, while others may provide additional insight into the game and its uniqueness. The following list is a composite of terms that will enhance understanding.

- **Ace**—A served ball that leads directly to a point for the serving team.
- **Attack**—The attempt by the offensive team to end play by hitting the ball to the floor of the defensive team.
- **Attack Block**—A defensive play that serves to angle the ball down onto the opponents' side of the court after it is contacted by an attacker.
- **Attack Line**—Line on the court parallel to the net and 3 m (10 ft) away from it.
- **Attacker**—A team player who spikes the ball in a downward trajectory (usually the team's final hit in the offensive play). Also referred to as a hitter or spiker.
- **Back Row Player**—A team member who has rotational position 1, 5, or 6 in the rotational order. The player may not jump to attack on or in front of the 3 m line when the ball is completely above the top of the net and may not participate in a block.
- **Block**—One, two, or three defensive players jumping in front of an attacker to prevent or slow down a spiked ball hit from the attack. Generally, the ball is contacted with the hands.
- **Blocker(s)**—The team player(s) responsible for blocking the attack. They may only be players in rotational positions 2, 3, and/or 4.
- **Body Line**—An imaginary line that runs from the top of the head through the base of the feet, bisecting the body vertically so two equal halves are formed.
- **Control Block**—An attempted block that slows down the speed of an attack so the back row players have an opportunity to play the ball.
- **Crosscourt**—An attack generated at an angle from one side of the attacking team's court to the opposite side of the defending team's court.

- **Dig**—Using a forearm pass or hand to play a ball that is in a low movement zone as a result of an attack.
- **Dink**—See **Tipping.**
- **Dive**—An emergency technique used when a player must extend the range of effectiveness. The player contacts the ball and then lands on the chest, abdomen, and thighs.
- **Down Ball**—An attacked ball that the blockers judge as lacking sufficient speed to require a block. The blockers shout "down ball" so that other team players can move to pass the ball to convert it into their offensive play.
- **Drifting**—Unnecessarily shifting the body laterally during takeoff in an airborne movement.
- **Emergency Technique**—A method to retrieve a ball that is outside the player's range of effectiveness. Examples include a dive and catch (the body), an extension roll, or a dive and slide.
- **Extension Roll**—An emergency technique where the ball is contacted in a low movement zone and out of body line. The result of contacting the ball out of body line is a roll that thrusts the feet over the shoulders so that the player is returned to the feet. Also referred to as a Japanese roll.
- **Floater Serve**—A method of putting the ball into play. The ball, once served with an overarm movement pattern, has little or no spin, thereby creating a "wiggling" effect through the air as it approaches the serve receiver.
- **Forearm Pass**—One of the basic skills in the game of volleyball. Any ball arriving at or below the player's waist can be easily passed using the forearms as the contacting surface.
- **Free Ball**—A ball returned by the opposing team that has little speed and high trajectory and can be played easily by the back row in order to set up a team attack.
- **High Seam**—Intentional attack of the ball between hands of two blockers.
- **Hit**—See **Attack.**
- **Hitter**—See **Attacker.**
- **Japanese Roll**—See **Extension Roll.**
- **Joust**—A ball held between opponents over the net. Play continues until the ball falls onto one side of the net or other. The team whose side the ball falls on will still have three contacts. If the ball goes out-of-bounds after the contact, the team on the opposite side of the net will be penalized.
- **Libero**—A defensive specialist who may substitute for any back court player.
- **Movement Zones**—Four basic areas of movement needed for movement in the game of volleyball: airborne, high, medium, and low.
- **Multiple Block (sometimes referred to as a composite block)**—Two or three players participating in the blocking attempt.
- **Offensive System**—A team's attack system that promotes the use of the team's strengths in specific situations; examples include 4-2; 5-1; 6-2.
- **Off-Speed Attack**—A spiked ball that has topspin but less than its maximum force.
- **Opening the Passing Lanes**—As the served ball travels toward the net, the

potential passers face the ball. As the ball passes over the net, all players not directly involved with the pass pivot and open toward the passer.

* **Overhead Pass**—One of the basic volleyball skills whereby a player contacts the ball with both hands simultaneously to control it and allow for continuation of the team's attack play.
* **Overlap**—A ruling based on foot placement of members of the receiving team as a ball is served. Adjacent players must keep their feet from completely crossing an imaginary dividing line, which would allow an unfair advantage for their team.

FIGURE 3.7 Ready position. Courtesy of USA Volleyball.

* **Rally**—The time from the serve initiation until play is ended by a point or point/sideout.
* **Rally Point Scoring**—A point is scored when either team wins the rally.
* **Range of Effectiveness**—Each player has a limited area on the court that can be easily reached. It extends in approximately a four-foot radius from the player's ready position.
* **Ready Position**—A position that is comfortable and suitable for the player to move from quickly in order to play a ball.
* **Rotational Order**—The right back position is considered as 1, right front is 2, middle front is 3, left front is 4, left back is 5, and middle back is 6. The rotational order must be maintained at the time of service.
* **Serve**—One of the basic volleyball skills. It is used to begin a game or put the ball in play.
* **Serve Receive**—A forearm pass generally used to direct the ball to the setter for the team's attack.
* **Serving Order**—See **Rotational Order**.
* **Set**—The overhead pass used as an offensive skill to direct the ball to an area where an attacker can contact the ball for the team's attack.
* **Sideout**—When the serving team loses the ball after a rally, the receiving team gets the ball.
* **Spike**—See **Attack**.
* **Spiker**—See **Attacker**.
* **Sprawl**—An emergency technique used when the player has reached completely forward and must extend parallel to the floor to play the ball.
* **Supportive Movement**—Movement by players who are not directly involved in playing the ball but, by body movement, assist in team communication.

- **Switching**—During the serve, players on the court may exchange positions, thereby moving into positions that best suit the offensive dynamics of their team.
- **Tempo**—Directing the ball at varying speeds and heights to facilitate the attack beating the block.
- **Tipping**—An off-speed attack in which the attacker gently places the ball behind or around the block. Also called **Dink.**
- **Trajectory**—Once airborne, the path of the body or the ball.
- **Underhand Serve**—Using an underhand movement pattern, the airborne ball may be put into play. Usually used with young players.
- **"W" Pattern**—A five-player service reception pattern; their court positions resemble the letter "W."
- **Wiping the Block**—An attacking technique that results in the ball rebounding out of the court off of the blockers' hands.

SUMMARY

- The sport of volleyball has one basic set of rules, with many groups providing specific modifications. The FIVB is the international governing body for volleyball; its rules are used by many countries and during international competition. In the United States, women's university rules are written by NAGWS. High school rules are written by the NFSHSA. All others are written by USA Volleyball.
- Pre-match protocol involves a specific way in which both teams share the entire playing area, with a designated amount of time on the court for each team separately and a designated time for shared use. After the introduction of teams and coaches, teams meet at center court and exchange small gifts and handshakes under the net.
- Prior to each serve, players must be in the correct rotational order in relation to their teammates. Once the ball is contacted for the serve, players may switch to anywhere on the court.
- A ball may be legitimately played with any body part. Brief contact, however, must occur.
- Players may not touch the net while playing the ball. Insignificant contact is not considered a fault. Reaching across the net is permitted during the follow through of an attack or when the offensive team has completed its attack and the defense is blocking. The block does not count as a contact. Blockers are permitted a second consecutive contact immediately after the block.
- Traditionally, a match may last from forty-five minutes to three hours. A match is three out of five games.
- Traditionally, each team is permitted two timeouts per game.
- The officiating team consists of the first referee, a second referee, two or four line judges, and an official scorekeeper.
- The basic skills of the game include the serve, the set, the attack, the block, and the dig.

- Fundamental volleyball terminology includes an ace, attack, block, dig, dive, down ball, serve, pass, free ball, joust, overlap, off-speed attack, rally, ready position, serve receive, rotational order, set, sideout, switching, and tipping.

▶ **pre-match protocol   p. 42**
Before a match, both teams warm up by rehearsing skills and sharing the entire playing area. The manner in which this process is completed is its protocol.

▶ **Rally Point Scoring   p. 43**
Each rally wins a point whether it is won by the serving or receiving team.

▶ **ball contact   p. 44**
Brief touch of the ball must occur and must be legitimately played using any part of the body.

▶ **play between the attack lines   p. 44**
cannot touch the net; reach across the net only during follow through of attack or when attack is complete; ball must pass over the net completely between the antennae; block does not count as a contact.

▶ **officiating team   p. 45**
the first referee; the second referee; others are two or four line judges, official scorekeeper.

▶ **basic skills of the game   p. 45**
serve, set, attack, block, dig.

▶ **Fundamental terminology   p. 47–50**

Assessment 3-1

Volleyball Match Analysis Assessment

Your Name _____

Teams: _____ v. _____

Game Scores: Game 1 _____ Game 2 _____ Game 3 _____

Game 4 _____ Game 5 _____

Before the match:

1. During the pre-match protocol, what responsibilities were conducted by the first referee? By the second referee? By the captains? By team members? By line judges?
2. Select a player to observe during the pre-match warmup. What behaviors were exhibited by the player during that time?

Throughout the match:

1. List 5 behaviors exhibited by the head coach of one of the teams. List 5 behaviors exhibited by an assistant coach. List 5 behaviors exhibited by a substitute. What similarities and uniquenesses did you observe in behaviors of these three people?
2. What offensive system was used by each team? How would you rate its success?
3. What defensive systems were used in conjunction with the opposing team's offensive systems? How would you rate their success?
4. What attack coverage was used by each team? How would you rate its success?
5. What type of block coverage was used by each team? How successful was it?
6. What specific volleyball skills did you observe each team using? How proficient were they in their performance?
7. Who was the setter(s) on each team? Who ran the plays for each team?

After the match:

1. What factors contributed to the victory of the winning team?
2. What factors contributed to the defeat of the other team?
3. What role did the substitutes play when entering the game related to momentum?
4. What was your perception of the contributions of the spectators to the match dynamics?
5. What would you have done differently if you were the coach of the team that won? The coach of the team that lost?

CHAPTER 4

PREPARING
TO PLAY
VOLLEYBALL

OBJECTIVES

After reading this chapter, you should be able to do the following:

*   Understand the physical, mental, and decision making components involved in playing volleyball.
*   Experience a flexibility and conditioning program designed for performance enhancement in volleyball.
*   Describe some of the basic workouts that prepare a player for success in the game.
*   Compose a nutritional regime that meets criteria necessary for quality performance.

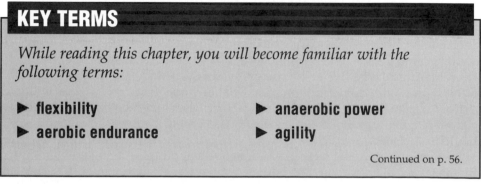

KEY TERMS

While reading this chapter, you will become familiar with the following terms:

▶ flexibility
▶ aerobic endurance

▶ anaerobic power
▶ agility

Continued on p. 56.

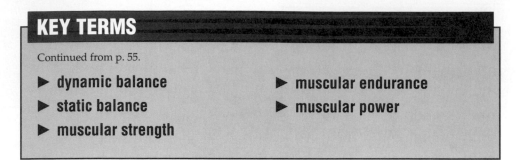

Continued from p. 55.

KEY TERMS

▶ **dynamic balance**
▶ **static balance**
▶ **muscular strength**

▶ **muscular endurance**
▶ **muscular power**

Volleyball is an explosive and dynamic sport. It requires repeated jumping, hitting, and quick movements in a variety of directions and movement zones. It also requires quick decision making that guides movement. A player must be agile, coordinated, balanced, strong, flexible, and possess adequate cardiovascular endurance to complete matches successfully. One key to improving performance in volleyball is to be adequately prepared physically. Other important keys to performing successfully in volleyball are appropriate nutrition, decision making, and biomechanical efficiency and effectiveness (volleyball-specific techniques).

PHYSICAL PERFORMANCE READINESS

Two general principles are important for improving physical performance. The first involves stress and the body's adaptation to stress, the stress-adaptation principle (SA). When the body is under physical stress, it changes or adapts to that stress. For example, if a conditioning program is devised that optimally stresses the body, then strength, endurance, flexibility, power, and so on, are increased.

Another principle is that of specificity of training. Generally, the more closely physical preparation resembles the actual demands required in the game, the more improved will be the resulting physical performance. This principle will be explored in more detail later.

Several components need to be considered when seeking improved physical performance. Warmup (increasing blood flow to muscles), flexibility (the range of motion within joints), agility (the ability to change directions quickly), aerobic/anaerobic fitness (the types of energy systems used by the body), muscular strength (the ability to perform maximally at any one time), power (the ability to perform maximally at a rapid rate), endurance (the ability to perform repeatedly without fatigue), and cool down (gradually decreasing the intensity of the activity) should be included.

Light jogging, jumping jacks, and light rope-skipping for three to five minutes are examples of elevating the body's temperature to prepare for volleyball (warmup). Gradually, blood begins to flow more rapidly to the muscles, nerve impulses travel more quickly, and the heart rate increases.

Because agility, muscular strength and endurance, power, and aerobic/anaerobic fitness are important components to success in the game, drills closely related to movements actually used in volleyball are vital. This idea is known as specificity of training. The theory of specificity is divided into two areas: (1) metabolic and (2) neuromuscular.

Metabolic specificity refers to the energy systems used by the body. Volleyball requires both aerobic (using oxygen) and anaerobic (without using oxygen) levels of fitness. Three different chemical reactions compose the energy systems used by the body: (1) the adenosine triphosphate-phosphocreatine (ATP-CP) system, (2) the lactic acid (LA) system, and (3) the oxygen (O_2) system. The first two systems require no additional use of oxygen, but the third does. Activities that enhance a combination of energy systems are beneficial. As a guide, the following time frames may be used to determine which energy system is being used if each player is working intensely throughout the time frame:

ATP-CP system—10 to 25 seconds
LA system—90 seconds to 3 minutes
O_2 system—3 to 5 minutes

Neuromuscular specificity deals with training the specific muscles which are actually used in playing the game. This means that in order to perform a spike most efficiently, a player should perform that movement repeatedly rather than substituting an overhand throw of a softball. Although many of the same muscle fibers may fire in both movements, the forces generated and the techniques used are quite different.

The following are examples of drills designed to improve skill levels by repeating similar volleyball movements (assisting in neuromuscular specificity) and also incorporating the use of various energy systems (assisting in metabolic specificity):

1. Three-player passing drill—Lateral movement
   Purpose: to develop lateral movement, ball control, and use of an energy system (dependent upon time frame selected)
   Description: See Figure 4-1.
2. The HANDS drill
   Purpose: to develop passing ability, backup movement, court awareness, agility, and use of an energy system (dependent upon time frame selected)
   Description: Players begin three on endline, three twelve feet behind endline; wall should be at least fifteen feet away from the endline. Captain tosses one ball to an area in front of each player. The player passes the ball to an area of the court where the setter is during a game.
      Immediately after passing the ball, the player backpedals and touches, with a hand, another player's hands. The player returns immediately and passes another volleyball. The groups rotate positions at the end of one minute. This format would primarily concentrate upon the LA energy system.
   Description: See Figure 4-2.

THREE-PLAYER PASSING—Lateral movement:

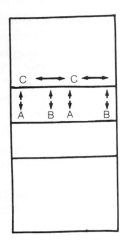

Purpose: To develop lateral movement and ball control.

Description: Players **A** and **B** are at the net, 10 feet apart, facing the endline. Player **C** is in the middle of the court in line with and facing **A**. **A** tosses the ball to **C** who passes back to **A** and side steps to be in line with **B**. **B** tosses the ball to **C** who passes back to **B**. **C** side steps back in line with **A**. To speed up the drill **A** and **B** should toss the ball as soon as **C** has passed the ball back to the other tosser.

Goals:
* Player **C**, who is passing, passes 10 to 30 balls. Players then rotate.

Variations:
* Instead of tossing, players **A** and **B** pass to player **C**. For this variation to be successful, all the players must have control.

FIGURE 4-1 Three-person passing drill. Courtesy of *Competitive Volleyball Drills for the Individual and Team.* Keller and Kluka, 1989.

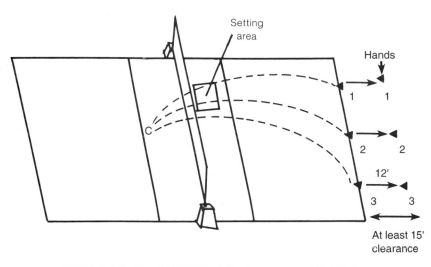

FIGURE 4-2 The HANDS drill. Courtesy of D. Kluka.

Cool down refers to a gradual decrease in the intensity of activity in order to adequately relax muscles and aid in injury prevention. Before leaving the volleyball area, light jogging for three to five minutes followed by five minutes of stretching the major muscle groups should help prepare the body for the rest of the day's activities.

It is important that all volleyball players begin by using total body exercises that will enhance overall physical fitness. By using a concept referred to as *functional con-*

ditioning, players can attain physical states that simulate body positions, postures, and movements that occur in game situations. Conditioning programs should include **agility, flexibility, aerobic endurance, anaerobic power, dynamic** and **static balance, muscular strength, muscular endurance,** and **muscular power.** These are components of movements which simulate those made in volleyball-specific skills.

For example, if a down-the-line attack is made from the left side of the court, the index finger of the hitting hand moves parallel with the sideline. Strength training that simulates a linear pattern would be appropriate. Frequently, however, the attack requires pointing the finger to the right sideline to cut the ball at a variety of angles and distances into the court. This type of movement involves rotator cuff muscles and connective tissue that must be strong enough to endure repeated use in varying degrees of angles, rotation, and distance.

The length and level of intensity of the program will increase as the program is continued. The program should be included within each day of practice. The program, based on beginning with three repetitions of each exercise, should be completed with as little rest as possible between exercises. Each set of exercises should be continued until fifteen can be successfully completed. It is important for repetitions to be held the same in each of the exercises. The goal for any functional conditioning program is to facilitate balance throughout the body. It is also important to "listen" to the body. When the body sends messages of overall fatigue, muscular tightening or cramping, or inefficient position, posture, or movement, it is time to stop the activity and rest.

Prior to any conditioning program, a few moments should be taken to mentally rehearse the body serving, setting, passing, attacking, blocking, and digging. Mentally rehearsing skills specific to the position being played is also useful. For example, a left side blocker/attacker might be rehearsing those movements while a defensive specialist might rehearse digging and passing. This type of rehearsal prepares the body for the upcoming events. By mentally focusing where the body is in space when performing each of the skills, imagining where the head is in relation to the center of mass (belly button), where the legs and arms are, and where the eyes are focused, the brain/body connections can begin to become integrated in the upcoming events of the conditioning program. The relationship between the head, trunk, and extremities (arms and legs) is important to improve posture, positioning, and balance during movement. It is, therefore, important to learn balanced movement in preparation for volleyball success.

ESTABLISHING NUTRITIONAL PRACTICES TO ENHANCE PERFORMANCE

There is no doubt that sound nutritional practice enhances volleyball performance, but the challenge lies in the practicing of nutritional behavior. Research shows that a carbohydrate-rich diet for volleyball players is best for providing the necessary energy for success. Foods that are high in complex carbohydrates include potatoes, breads, pastas, rice, cereal, vegetables (e.g., carrots and corn), and dried beans. Whole grain foods provide B vitamins, which act as catalysts to metabolize energy. Simple carbohydrates include fruits such as watermelon, grapes, and raisins; honey; sugar; and soft drinks. These provide a steady stream of energy and can be used for snacks and instant energy. Completing meals should be a wide variety of foods, particularly those that represent nuts, meats, fish, and poultry. Nuts and dried beans also provide carbohydrates. They also provide a rich source of fat. Dairy foods, such as cheese and eggs, also provide carbohydrates. Protein and calcium are also present and provide nutrients for growth and tissue repair.

The following foods are representative of major food groups that are important for performance enhancement in volleyball. Leafy vegetables—5 servings; milk/cheese—3 servings; bread/cereal/rice/pasta—11 servings; meat/poultry/fish/eggs/nuts—3 servings; fruits—4 servings.

Eating the appropriate foods daily can lead to improved performance. A strategy of balanced energy intake through natural food use can facilitate energy and wellness. With this type of nutritional balance, a lifestyle involving appropriate food intake can serve as a solid basis for healthy, lifelong eating habits.

SUMMARY

- Volleyball is an explosive and dynamic sport. It requires repeated jumping, hitting, and quick movements in a variety of directions and movement zones. It also requires quick decision making that guides movement. A player must be agile, coordinated, balanced, strong, flexible, and possess adequate cardiovascular endurance to complete matches successfully.
- Several components need to be considered when seeking improved physical performance: warmup, flexibility, agility, aerobic/anaerobic/fitness, power, endurance, and cool down.
- Functional conditioning can provide excellent training to provide readiness for the game. Circuit training can provide volleyball players with conditioning exercises in a continuous and timed program that works volleyball-specific muscle groups as well as developing an aerobic energy base necessary for games and matches.
- Sound nutritional practice enhances volleyball performance as well. A carbohydrate-rich diet is best for providing the necessary energy for success. A strategy of balanced energy intake through natural food use can facilitate energy and wellness.
- Volleyball skill acquisition has at least three components for success: (1) information gathered by the player through the visual system; (2) perceptual decision-making strategies developed through the visual system/brain connection; and (3) efficient and effective movement production resulting from the visual system/brain/body connection. Effective quick action plans are based on three skills: visual search, selective attention, and anticipation.

▶ **flexibility**   p. 59
the range of motion within joints

▶ **aerobic endurance**   p. 59
the ability to perform repeatedly without cardiovascular fatigue; the use of an oxygen-based energy system

▶ **anaerobic power**   p. 59
the ability to perform maximally at a rapid rate; the use of an energy system without oxygen as its base

▶ **agility**   p. 59
the ability to change directions quickly while balancing speed and body control

▶ **dynamic balance**   p. 59
performing a movement in space that is in control; adjusting the body's center of mass throughout the movement

▶ **static balance**   p. 59
holding a posture or position in space that is in control; keeping the body's center of mass steady

▶ **muscular strength**   p. 59
the ability to perform maximally at any one time

▶ **muscular endurance**   p. 59
the ability to perform repeatedly without muscular fatigue

▶ **muscular power**   p. 59
the ability to generate a maximum force in the shortest amount of time

Assessment 4-1

Name   Section   Date

Step 1: Using a graph computer application program, devise graphs of the following information. Based upon the visual representation of the information below, summarize and analyze the teams' profiles and compare/contrast males and females at the elite level.

Women's Teams—Average Height, Spike Touch, and Block Touch

	Height	Spike Touch	Block Touch
Brazil	6'0" (182.9 cm)	9'11" (302.3 cm)	9'4" (284.5 cm)
China	6'0" (182.9 cm)	10'3" (312.4 cm)	9'9" (297.2 cm)
Cuba	5'10" (177.8)	10'8" (325.1 cm)	10'3" (312.4 cm)
Germany	6'1" (185.4 cm)	10'1" (307.3 cm)	9'5" (287 cm)
Japan	5'10" (177.8 cm)	9'11" (302.3 cm)	9'5" (287 cm)
Korea	5'10" (177.8 cm)	10'0" (304.8 cm)	9'6" (289.6 cm)
Peru	5'10" (177.8 cm)	9'11" (302.3 cm)	9'2" (279.4 cm)
Russia	6'2" (182.9 cm)	10'0" (304.8 cm)	9'10" (299.7 cm)
USA	6'0" (183.3 cm)	10'0" (304.8 cm)	9'8" (294.6 cm)
USA Youth National	6'0" (182.9 cm)	9'9" (297.2 cm)	9'5" (287 cm)
USA Junior National	6'1" (182.9 cm)	9'10" (299.7 cm)	9'6" (289.6 cm)

Men's Teams—Average Height, Spike Touch, and Block Touch

	Height	Spike Touch	Block Touch
Brazil	6'5" (195.6 cm)	11'1" (337.8 cm)	10'5" (317.5 cm)
Bulgaria	6'6" (198.1 cm)	11'2" (340.4 cm)	10'8" (325.3 cm)
China	6'5" (195.6 cm)	11'6" (350.5 cm)	11'0" (335.7 cm)
Cuba	6'5" (195.6 cm)	11'7" (353.1 cm)	11'1" (337.8 cm)
Czech Republic	6'6" (198.1 cm)	11'3" (342.9 cm)	10'9" (327.7 cm)
Italy	6'5" (195.6 cm)	11'4" (345.4 cm)	10'4" (315 cm)
Netherlands	6'6" (198.1 cm)	11'2" (340.4 cm)	10'6" (320 cm)
Russia	6'6" (198.1 cm)	11'5" (348 cm)	11'0" (335.3 cm)
Ukraine	6'6" (198.1 cm)	11'3" (342.9 cm)	10'9" (327.7 cm)
USA	6'6" (198.1 cm)	11'5" (348 cm)	10'8" (325.1 cm)
USA Youth National	6'4" (193 cm)	10'8" (325.1 cm)	10'0" (304.8 cm)
USA Junior National	6'6" (198.1 cm)	11'1" (337.8 cm)	10'4" (315 cm)

Step 2: Determine your height, your spike touch, and your block touch. Determine how you compare to the information listed above. Working with a partner, your height can be determined by using a tape measure applied to a wall so that when you stand, facing away from the wall, your partner can appropriately take a measurement. Your spike touch is assessed by taking your spike approach, jumping, swinging and touching the wall. Your block touch is assessed by taking one step, jumping, and contracting the wall. The measurement where you have touched the wall is what is recorded.

Assessment 4-2

An Integrated Conditioning Program

Name   Section   Date

Record the length of time it takes for you to complete the sequences below. Perform portions of this sample program prior to beginning your class each day.

Once focused on the task at hand, a program that integrates flexibility, strength, power, and endurance can be your performance success. The following program has been devised as an example of *functional conditioning* for volleyball.

Warmup: Beginning at the left back corner of the court, jog around the outside of the court once clockwise, once counterclockwise, and once diagonally forward to the right front corner, across the length of the net, and diagonally backward to the right back corner. This brief warmup provides increased blood flow to muscles and connective tissue in the arms and legs. Concentrate on keeping the head and trunk balanced over the center of mass while jogging. Keep the eyes focused straight ahead while jogging.

Initial posture:
Stand with head in front of center of mass, and look straight ahead; trunk and knees should be slightly flexed, hands on outside of legs at knee height, and keep feet flat on the floor and shoulder width apart.

Sequence One:

1. Perform ankle circles clockwise; counterclockwise; figure 8s.
2. Perform knee circles clockwise; counterclockwise; figure 8s.
3. With the knees flexed at 120 degrees, perform knee circles clockwise; counterclockwise; figure 8s.
4. With the knees flexed at 90 degrees, perform knee circles clockwise; counterclockwise; figure 8s.
5. With the knees flexed at 90 degrees, perform hip circles clockwise; counterclockwise; figure 8s.

Stand up, stretch for the ceiling with the hands, and drop head back to look at ceiling while stretching.

Initial posture:
Stand with head in front of center of mass, and look straight ahead; trunk and knees should be slightly flexed, hands on outside of legs at knee height, keep feet flat on the floor and shoulder width apart.

Sequence Two:

1. Pull elbows back of the body; pull elbows laterally, away from the body; pull elbows up in front of the body.
2. With straight arms, cross arms in front of the body with thumbs up; cross arms in front of the body with thumbs down; cross arms in front of the body with thumbs pointing laterally (away from the belly button).
3. Arm circles to the side with thumbs up; arm circles to the side with thumbs down; arm circles to the side with thumbs pointing out and horizontal to the floor; arm circles to the side with thumbs pointing in and horizontal to the floor.

Stand up, stretch for the ceiling with the hands, and drop head back to look at ceiling while stretching.

Initial posture:

Stand with head in front of center of mass, and look straight ahead; trunk and knees should be slightly flexed, hands on outside of legs at knee height, feet flat on the floor and shoulder width apart.

Sequence Three:

1. Shoulder shrug up and down; shoulders forward and shoulders back; shoulder circles forward; shoulder circles backward.
2. Interlock the fingers and place the palms of the hands on the forehead and repeat #1.

Stand up, stretch for the ceiling with the hands, and drop head back to look at ceiling while stretching.

Initial posture:

Flex trunk, knees, and ankles until finger tips touch floor, with feet shoulder width apart and weight on the balls of the feet.

Sequence Four:

1. Shift weight from the balls of the feet to the finger tips; shift weight toward heels and slowly extend knees.
2. Place toes in an inward position; repeat the above.
3. Place toes in an outward position; repeat the above.

Initial posture:

Feet on the floor, widened side-to-side stance twice that of shoulder width; hands on the outside of the legs at knee height; look straight ahead.

Sequence Five:

1. Shift weight over right foot, then over left foot; circles to the right; circles to the left; figure 8s.
2. Repeat Sequence Four from the widened stance position.

Initial posture:

Stand facing a wall, and place the forearms against the wall by learning in to the wall while keeping heels on the floor.

Sequence Six:

1. Flex the knees; as knees flex, arms slide down the wall.
2. Repeat #1, with toes inward; with toes outward.
3. Repeat #1, standing on one foot; then standing on the other foot.

Initial posture:

Stand looking straight ahead, with feet together.

Sequence Seven:

1. Bring one knee up to chest and step forward into a lunge position, landing on the ball of the foot; lower the torso toward the floor, flexing the front knee to 90 degrees; repeat on the other side of the body.
2. Bring one knee up to chest and step backward into a lunge position, landing on the ball of the foot; lower the torso toward the floor, flexing the back knee to 90 degrees; repeat on the other side of the body.
3. Bring one knee up to chest and step laterally into a lunge position, landing on the ball of the foot; lower the torso toward the floor, flexing the original knee to 90 degrees; repeat on the other side of the body.

Initial posture:

Take push-up position with feet dropped below the trunk.

Sequence Eight:

1. Complete push-ups with hands placed shoulder width apart and fingers pointing forward to a point where elbows are at 90 degrees in the downward phase of the push-up. Complete pushups with hands twice shoulder width apart and fingers pointing forward where elbows are at 90 degrees. Complete pushups with thumbs and index fingers touching at chest sternum height on the floor where elbows are at 90 degrees.

Assessment 4-3

Name   Section   Date

It is also important for volleyball players to possess sufficient flexibility to maximize their performance and reduce the opportunity for injury. Although there are no definitive measurements available as to the appropriate amount of flexibility necessary to prevent injury, several markers can be used to determine minimal flexibility measurements. For example, mobility of the ankles, knees, hips, trunk, and shoulders are important.

If the player feels tension in the legs, trunk, and/or shoulder areas, there is a clear indication that the player needs to work on flexibility in those areas. Lateral trunk rotation should minimally be at 45 degrees, while the shoulder should be from 30 to 45 degrees without rotating the trunk.

Flexibility increases quickness of muscular contraction/relaxation, and helps prevent injury. The following exercises are samples that could be incorporated into a five-minute period. (NOTE: When stretching, go slowly, gently, and consistently. DO NOT BOUNCE. Bouncing may tear muscle fibers.)

1. Bent knee stretch
   Muscles: lower back and hamstrings
   Directions: Grab ankles and pull until you feel the stretch.
               Hold six seconds and relax. Repeat three times.
2. Torso stretch
   Muscles: trunk and legs
   Directions: Lying on the back with arms horizontal on the floor, place the right leg on the floor across the body so that it is parallel with the left arm (Figure 4-3 [2]). Change sides. Repeat three times per side.
3. Leg pull
   Muscles: hamstrings, gluteal (rear), and lower back muscles
   Directions: Pull both legs toward chest.
               Feel stretch in hamstrings and gluteals.
               Hold six seconds and relax. Repeat three times.
4. Shoulder stretch
   Muscles: shoulder girdle area
   Directions: Pull arms of partner back until partner discomfort occurs.
               Hold for six seconds and relax. Repeat three times.

5. Calf stretch
    Muscles: gastrocnemius, Achilles tendon
    Calf stretch
    Directions: Stand, with one foot in front of the other.
    Lean forward, keeping heel on the floor.
    Hold for six seconds and relax.
    Repeat three times. Change lead leg.

(1) Bent Knee Stretch

(2) Torso Stretch. Courtesy of D. Kluka.

(3) Leg Pull. Courtesy of D. Kluka.

(4) Shoulder Stretch.
Courtesy of D. Kluka.

(5) Calf Stretch.
Courtesy of D. Kluka.

FIGURE 4-3(1–5) Sample flexibility exercises.

Assessment 4-4

Circuit Training Approach

Name _____   Section _____   Date _____

Circuit training can provide volleyball players with conditioning exercises in a continuous and timed program that works volleyball-specific muscle groups as well as developing an aerobic energy base necessary for games and matches. By using the circuit approach, basic strength and speed training, movement and agility work, and an aerobic base can be integrated efficiently. A circuit can be conducted three days a week, building up to three completions of circuit stations within 45 minutes. Use a 15-second exercise and a 15-second recovery within each station; begin the next station within 15 seconds after completion of the previous one. Below is an example of a 8-station circuit that can be used to enhance performance parameters.

Record your success upon completion of the above sequence. Perform this as part of your conditioning program throughout the course.

Station 1—Jump Rope

Starting position: stand, holding the rope in both hands; place the rope behind the body to begin.

Exercise: Jump the rope with one jump per revolution of the rope, emphasizing height in each jump. To emphasize jumping height, land on the balls of the feet each time.

Sequence: Jump; jump; rest; jump; rest; jump; rest; jump; rest; rest; jump; jump; move to the next station.

Station 2—Volleyball Throw from a Standing Position

Starting position: stand, facing 10' away from a wall; hold the volleyball with the hitting hand.

Exercise: Using a full arm swing, throw the ball high against the wall, engaging hip, shoulder, elbow, and wrist involvement to generate force; catch the ball when it rebounds.

Sequence: 12 throws; rest; 12 throws; rest; move to the next station.

Station 3—Progressive Sprints the Length of the Court

Starting position: sprint position behind an endline.

Exercise: On the outside portion of the court, run at varying speeds from endline to endline; jog another 10 feet; return to second endline.

Sequence: sprint at 50%; sprint at 25%; sprint at 75%; rest; sprint at 100%; sprint at 50%; sprint at 100%; rest; sprint at 100%; sprint at 25%; rest; move to the next station.

71

Station 4—Square Agility

Starting position: defensive position, starting on the intersection of the cross taped on the floor (+).

Exercise: Without crossing the feet, keep hips forward throughout the exercise; move forward and touch front tape with both hands; move to starting position; move back and touch back line with both hands; move to starting position; move to right and touch right line with near hand; move to starting position; move to left and touch left line with near hand; move to starting position. Repeat the sequence throughout the time frame; move to the next station.

Station 5—Volleyball Throw from a Kneeling Position

Starting position: kneeling on a mat, facing a wall, 10′ away; volleyball held in both hands, behind head so that elbows are even with the ears

Exercise: Allow the ball to go behind the head as far as possible, then throw the ball as rapidly as possible to the wall by snapping the wrists; catch the ball as it rebounds.

Sequence: 12 throws; rest; 12 throws; rest; move to the next station.

Station 6—Jump Rope for Speed

Starting position: stand, holding the rope in both hands; place the rope behind the body to begin.

Exercise: Jump the rope with one jump per revolution of the rope, emphasizing speed of the rope. To emphasize jumping speed, land on the balls of the feet each time and keep the amount of space between the feet and the floor as small as possible.

Sequence: Jump; rest; jump; jump; rest; jump; jump; rest; jump; jump; rest; move to the next station.

Station 7—Court-length Sprints

Starting position: sprint position behind an endline

Exercise: on the outside portion of the court, sprint from endline to endline; jog another 10 feet; return to the second endline.

Sequence: sprint; sprint; rest; sprint; rest; sprint; rest; sprint; rest; sprint; sprint; sprint; move to the next station.

Station 8—Scissor Jumps

Starting position: forward lunge

Exercise: Jump forcefully upward, using the arms to drive, and scissor the legs so that the back one becomes the front one; upon landing, jump, and scissor again; keep the back straight and focus the eyes straight ahead.

Sequence: 6 jumps; rest; 6 jumps; rest; 6 jumps; rest; 6 jumps; rest; 6 jumps; rest; 6 jumps; rest; move to the next station.

Assessment 4-5

Carbohydrate Count

Name   Section   Date

Determine the approximate number of carbohydrates needed for daily training diet. Multiply 3 × pounds of body weight to equal the grams of carbohydrate needed.

Assessment 4-6

Name _____ Section _____ Date _____

Determine a menu for yourself for three days, following the guidelines included in this chapter. Use the food record provided below to record food to be consumed.

FOOD RECORD

Name _____ Dates _____

Time	Food/Drink	Quantity	Category

Assessment 4-7

Name   Section   Date

There is increasing evidence that volleyball skill acquisition has at least three components for success: (1) information gathered by the player through the visual system; (2) perceptual decision-making strategies developed through the visual system/brain connection; and (3) efficient and effective movement production resulting from the visual system/brain/body connection.

Generally, there is a core of visual/perceptual skills needed to optimize success in volleyball: (1) acuity (dynamic and static); (2) vergence (convergence/divergence); (3) dynamic stereopsis; (4) central/peripheral awareness; (5) glare recovery; (6) contrast sensitivity function; (7) fusion; (8) color perception; and (9) total reaction time.

Equipment: one piece of string 12 to 15 feet long, 1/8 inch in diameter

Description: Attach one end of the string to the top of a door. Wrap the other end around the index finger of your hitting hand. Pull the string taut so that your index finger touches the tip of your nose.

Assessment: (1) Focus at the far end of the string. You should see a "V" that begins at the top of the door. Visualize a mini volleyball slowing rolling down the string toward your nose. When the "ball" arrives halfway down the string, you should see an "X". Then visualize the "ball" going slowly back up to the top of the door. The string will appear to wave or ripple. (2) After focusing continuously down and up the string, focus on the far end of the string. Then focus on the middle of the string; then one foot in front of your finger; then to the end of the string, the middle, and one foot in front of your finger. (3) Focus at the far end of the string; follow the string down to one foot in front of your finger; follow the string back to the far end of the string.

Assessment 4-8

Name   Section   Date

Effective quick action plans are based on three skills: visual search, selective attention, and anticipation. Appropriate visual search strategies are initially comprised of four types of eye movements which, when combined, gather information for decision making: saccadic, vestibulo-ocular, vergence, and smooth pursuit. For example, when playing Libero, the player watches the play develop as the ball travels across the net to the first pass (vergence and smooth pursuit), then tracks the ball toward the setter's hands (smooth pursuit), then checks potential attackers (saccadic), and locks in on the ball just before it is hit, while maintaining dynamic balance (vestibulo-ocular). As the ball is hit, its velocity can approach speeds of 100 mph, producing angular velocities in excess of 500 degrees per second. The Libero views the ball distinctly for the last time at attack contact (smooth pursuit).

After successful use of visual search strategies, attentional focus also helps the player devise a quick action plan. Attention has been categorized into four styles: broad internal, broad external, narrow internal, and broad internal. Generally, reading and recognizing bits of information occur using broad external focus. Players must learn to zoom out externally (read), zoom in externally (intensely read), produce a controlled contact (narrow internal), and produce scoring contact based on a broad internal focus. Those players who learn to anticipate or determine the likelihood that in certain conditions, certain things will occur can devise quick action plans for performance success.

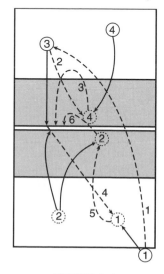

Description: Player 1 serves the ball over the net to Player 3, and Player 1 transitions from serving to defense. Player 3 passes the ball to the center front position. Player 4 goes to the center front position to set the ball back to Player 3. Player 3 spikes the ball to Player 1. Player 1 digs the ball while Player 2 moves to set the ball back to Player 1. Player 1 approaches and spikes to Player 4. The drill continues. Focus should zoom out externally, zoom in externally, controlled contact narrow internally, and scoring contact based on a broad and internal focus.

FIGURE 4-4

CHAPTER 5

BASICS OF **PASSING**

OBJECTIVES

After reading this chapter, you should be able to do the following:

* Perform the forearm pass; the overhead pass (front and back); read and dig; diving, rolling, or sprawling.
* Describe the basic components of forearm passing; overhead passing; reading and digging; diving, rolling, and sprawling.
* Understand the strategic use of each of these skills.

KEY TERMS

While reading this chapter, you will become familiar with the following terms:

▶ assertive movement   ▶ forward movement

▶ supportive movement   ▶ lateral movement

▶ movement zones   ▶ body line

▶ ready position   ▶ balancing the court

Continued on p. 82.

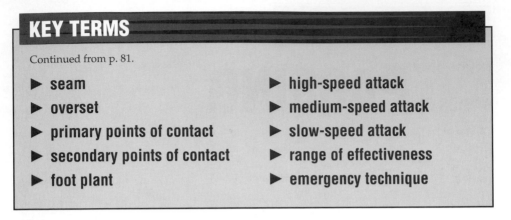

Continued from p. 81.

► seam
► overset
► primary points of contact
► secondary points of contact
► foot plant

► high-speed attack
► medium-speed attack
► slow-speed attack
► range of effectiveness
► emergency technique

In order to facilitate passing techniques, an understanding of basic movement is vital.

The game of volleyball has the smallest playing surface area of any team sport. The playing area is limited by boundary lines and a net; the net divides the total surface area in half. Six players must move on one-half of the court, while six more move on the other half. This creates two unique situations: (1) a crowded area for movement and (2) a limited time to react.

Movements must be efficient, accurate, and appropriately timed with the speed of the ball. A spiked ball, rebounding from the hitter's hand and landing on the endline, can travel the distance within one-half second.

Additionally, movement must be **assertive.** One of the greatest communicators on the court is body movement (or lack of it). **Supportive movement,** or movement by players who are not directly involved in playing the ball, is the primary method of communication. Since communication is the sharing of meanings, it is critical that all players share the movement terminology.

Because the complexion of the game changes rapidly from offense to defense, appropriate body movement depends upon the game situation and the technique used. There are four basic **movement zones:**

1. airborne—used in spiking, blocking, jump setting, jump serving;
2. high—used in serving, initial zone of movement for blocking, setting;
3. medium—used in forearm passing, serve reception, overhand passing, initial zone of movement for the approach in spiking; and
4. low—used in digging and emergency techniques, including diving and rolling.

The **medium zone of movement** is the most frequently used zone in the game of volleyball. It is a "waiting" position while the play is developing. Each medium movement is begun from the basic **ready position.** This position permits a variety of body movement possibilities quickly. Forward, backward, and lateral movements are frequently used within preparatory and supportive movement. Important aspects of the ready position include placing the feet slightly wider than shoulder width apart, with the right foot slightly ahead if the player is closer to the right sideline and the left foot ahead if the player is closer to the left sideline. This foot placement will assist in balance, help to keep the hips angled into the court so that the ball's trajectory is within the playing area when contacted, and assure that movement is directed toward the ball. Weight is distributed on the inside and the balls of the feet rather than on the outside. The knees are slightly flexed and in front of the feet. Shoulders are in front of the knees. The back is straight, and the arms and hands are positioned between the waist and knees. The palms of the hands are facing each other in front of the body.

Forward movement in the medium zone is movement toward the ball in a forward direction. Feet, hips, knees, shoulders, and head/eyes point toward the direction of movement and are centered behind the ball.

FIGURE 5-1 Basic ready position. Courtesy of D. Kluka.

Just before ball contact is made, the feet, hips, knees, shoulders, and head/eyes pivot (if necessary) and point to the target area where the ball is to go. Forward movement can be effectively used during serve reception, in the spike approach, and in the preparation phase of the block.

Forward movement toward an endline or sideline may also be used to reach a ball that cannot be contacted within one or two steps. The difficulty, however, is that the target area is generally toward the net; this places the body in an inefficient

Checklist 1

Ready Position

Look at Figure 5-1. The man is in the basic ready position. Answer these questions in the checklist based on his body position.

	YES	NO
• Feet slightly wider apart than the shoulders?		
• Weight distributed on inside and balls of feet?		
• Knees slightly flexed and in front of toes?		
• Arms and hands positioned between waist and knees?		
• Palms of hands facing each other in front of body?		

position to play the ball successfully. Sideline and endline forward movements should be used as emergency techniques only.

Backward medium movement is primarily used when facing the net. Once a play on the ball or a supportive movement is made, backward movement is used to return to a neutral area on the court.

Lateral movement is movement to the side to keep the midline of the body directly behind the ball when contacted. It is stepping to the side using a step and a jump to a stop before playing the ball. From the ready position, a step is taken in the direction of the movement desired. Just prior to ball contact, a low, quick jump to a stop is performed, keeping feet shoulder width apart during the jump. The step and jump to a stop in volleyball is the bringing of both feet off the floor and landing on them simultaneously in order to attain a stable position from which to pass the ball.

A high zone of movement is an extended body position, the feet still in contact with the ground. Standing tall and reaching toward the ball with the hitting hand during any act of service is an example of efficiency in the high movement zone. It is important to note that, although body parts are moving during the performance of any skill, the feet are stationary.

To achieve movement in the airborne zone, other zones of movement have played integral parts. In blocking, medium and high movement zones combine to establish airborne movement. The objective, once airborne, is to maximize height and minimize lateral movement.

Movement in the low zone generally begins in a medium posture. Emergency techniques are those that require the total body to make contact with the floor. Once the body is dropped to the low zone, it can easily glide to the floor.

Supportive movements are those performed prior to ball contact by team members other than those directly involved in the play. Because of these movements of

FIGURE 5-2 A dink around a single block, both in the airborne zone. Courtesy of Richard Bajjalien.

FIGURE 5-3 Movement to the ball in a low zone. Courtesy of D. Kluka.

support, players' court space responsibilities fluctuate with each play. Areas or zones of responsibility change in size, shape, and court location. Responsibilities for critical zones of the court must be given during each play, depending upon team court coverage. This is termed **balancing the court.** The court is balanced by dividing the zone between players by size of available space and according to the weakness within the zone.

Communication is essential during supportive movements used to balance the court. Prior to each series of plays, a brief discussion needs to occur between adjacent players on the court. The most vulnerable areas are those where zones overlap or where there is a **seam.** For example, while playing defense in the right back position, the player must communicate that those balls traveling below the waist and/or behind are in the zone of responsibility covered by the middle back.

To enhance ball contact within movement zones and areas of responsibilities, several general concepts need to be emphasized:

- Body weight should be balanced between the feet. This will allow for greater opportunities to move in any direction to play the ball.
- All movement should begin toward the ball. This can be done by moving the feet first. By doing this, the body can be kept in dynamic balance.
- Body position should be open so the ball's position is between the body and the net. This will allow movement to the ball and in the direction of the flow of the game, back court to front court.
- Body parts need to be stabilized at ball contact. If using a forearm pass, the body is firmly planted in the position as the ball rebounds from the arms.
- Whatever techniques are used to contact the ball, presentation of the appropriate surface area as soon as possible will enhance play on the ball.
- Ball contact should be made in **body line.** If a photograph is taken as the ball is contacted, the ball's position would divide the player's body so that half would appear to the right of it and half to the left of it.
- In addition to contacting the ball in body line, the player directs feet, hips, shoulders, and head/eyes toward the target area.

Eye movements can also be considered as basic in volleyball play. Their movement is critical to the processing of information, an important aspect of playing the game successfully. Because of a rapidly changing environment, a player must quickly, accurately, and continuously select sources of visual information during play. Prior to the beginning of a game, each player should walk around the perimeter of the court, looking for reference points on the ceiling relative to boundary lines. These reference points are critical as they can give the player information by which to decide if a ball is in bounds without changing focus from the ball to the boundary lines.

Eye movement should always be focused upon a specific point on the ball as it contacts any striking surface. The smaller the area of visual concentration, the less chance for error when the ball is contacted. Once the ball has rebounded into the air, its trajectory cannot be altered. The eyes can freely scan the court between contacts. The more rapid the eye movements, the more information is available for processing. Relevant information gathered through scanning will assist in faster decision making during the developing play as well.

There may be situations, however, that could require the eyes to continue to follow the ball. After a spiker has attacked the ball or a blocker has contacted the ball, its rebound will be tremendously quick. Focusing upon the ball until the next contact will increase time for anticipation and reaction. As a result, each player should have more time to select a movement, position the body for ball contact, or offer supportive movement. For additional detailed information, See Appendix C.

FOREARM PASS

Forearm passing is the key to the beginning of any team's offensive system. It is generally a team's first contact and assists in reducing the speed of the ball when passing to the setter. Preparation for ball contact is critical to the success of the forearm pass. The step and jump to a stop discussed in the Basic Movement section of this chapter enhances the stability of the platform from which the ball is passed.

GENERAL FOREARM PASS CONCEPTS

- The larger the base of support, the more stable the body becomes. The body should be in a statically balanced position just prior to ball contact. Keeping the feet wider than the shoulders at contact provides greater body stability. Movement away from the midline of the body in any one direction will cause the body's center of gravity to shift in that direction, throwing it into an unbalanced position.
- To create a stable platform, the arms are extended from the shoulders and in front of the body.
- The forearm pass involves rebounding the ball off of the forearm. The ball will rebound at the angle from which it is hit but in the opposite vertical and/or horizontal direction. If the passing platform is horizontal, the ball will rebound straight up in the air.

From the ready position, movement is made to the ball by one, two, or a series of quick steps. The feet stop in a staggered position by hopping to the ball in the direction of the target. Movement is in the medium zone. The right foot is slightly forward, pointing toward the target. Once stopped, the shoulders are forward; the palms of the hands are brought together in front of the body so that a firm platform is formed by the extended arms; and the arms are parallel to the thighs. The fingertips of the hands are angled downward toward the floor, while the thumbs are adjacent and parallel to one another.

The ball is contacted slightly closer to the wrists than to the elbows on the forearms. Its rebound is simultaneous from both forearms and in body line. Upon contact, weight is shifted from back to front leg, with movement going toward the target. Arm movement is directly proportional to the speed of the ball at contact. A high-speed hit may require the passer to freeze the follow-through. A serve may demand a slight lifting movement at contact. The angle at which the ball is

FIGURE 5-4 Forearm pass sequence. Courtesy of Clint Carlton.

Checklist 2

Forearm Pass		
	YES	NO
• From the ready position, quick movement to the ball?		
• Once stopped, feet in a stride position?		
• Knees bent?		
• Shoulder forward and back straight?		
• Palms of hands together to form a platform with arms fully extended?		
• Fingers point toward floor?		
• Thumbs adjacent and parallel to one another?		
• Platform slanted toward target?		
• Eyes focused on ball at contact?		
• Ball played in body line at contact?		
• Weight shifted from back to front leg during follow through?		
• Arms extended during follow through?		
• Arms not higher than shoulders?		
• Eyes follow ball to target?		

contacted will largely determine its angle of rebound: the higher the platform, the higher the ball's trajectory.

It is critical for the passer to focus on the ball while it is approaching. The more times the eyes can focus on the ball throughout its approach, the more successful will be the body position for the pass. The ball should be seen contacting the forearms; focus should be continued as it leaves to see its flight pattern. Once its trajectory has been identified, information about the developing play can be gained by scanning.

The forearm pass is used as *the* preferred passing technique in serve reception. The objective is to pass the ball where the setter has a variety of options. Back court players receive approximately three-fourths of all balls successfully served. This technique can prevent points or make points for the opponents. The quality of the technique definitely makes a difference.

OVERHEAD PASS: FRONT; BACK

The overhead pass is generally employed to redirect the ball with the most accuracy offered by any skill in volleyball. It is most frequently used by a setter as a team's second contact. The setter "places" a ball above waist level so an attacker can effectively hit the ball into the opponents' court.

GENERAL OVERHEAD PASSING CONCEPTS

FIGURE 5-5 Overhead pass position without the ball. Courtesy of C. Carlton.

- Coming to a stationary position before the ball arrives assists in providing stability and time to assess the situation.
- When body parts move, the location of the center of gravity in the body shifts. It is therefore important that, as the ball approaches, the ready position is assumed. All movement is then made through the ball and in the direction of its intended flight.
- For greatest accuracy, the ball should be contacted when the hands are at an angle to the intended target. For an overhead pass from the right side of the court for a middle attack, the ball is passed at a more vertical angle, perhaps 75 degrees. For a pass going from the right side to the left side of the court, the ball is redirected at up to a 45 degree angle.
- When functioning as a setter for the attack, overhead pass the ball between the attacker and the net. This provides the attacker with the option of adjusting to make successful contact.

FIGURE 5-6 Hand positioning on the ball (back view). Courtesy of D. Kluka.

FIGURE 5-7 Hand positioning on ball (front view). Courtesy of D. Kluka.

The accuracy of the pass depends upon the absorption of the ball and its height. The objective of the front overhead pass is to absorb the force coming into the hands and fingers while projecting and redirecting the ball to a target area along and above the net. To accomplish this objective, the player must get into position rapidly in order to make the best choices. Once in a balanced position under the ball and in body line so the ball is approaching the forehead, the feet should be in a staggered

Checklist 3

Overhead Passing		
	YES	NO
• A balanced position rapidly moving hands and elbows up?		
• Feet staggered and weight evenly distributed with knees slightly bent, trunk upright?		
• At contact, lower back of ball, absorbed by the hands, making hands move backward?		
• Legs, hips, arms, and hands push the ball outward and extend?		
• Feet remain in contact with the floor throughout ball contact?		
• Weight transferred toward target?		

position approximately shoulder width apart; the right foot is ahead of the left when in front of the 3 m line so the hips are open to the approaching pass. If the pass occurs around the 3 m line, the feet should be even; if the pass is behind the 3m line, the left foot should be forward. This also assists in keeping the overhead pass from being **overset** onto the opponents' side of the net. The knees should be slightly flexed so that the body is in the medium zone of movement; the upper body is upright.

The more quickly both hands get to the overhead passing position, the more time there will be available to make good attack decisions. The triceps of the arms are parallel to the floor. The hands are shaped so they conform to the surface of the ball. The thumbs are in line with and about six inches from the pupils of the eyes, pointing to each respective eye; the ball is focused upon through the window created by the thumbs and index fingers. If a change of focus were made, the thumb nails would be clearly seen instead of the ball. **Primary points of contact** are those that supply the power. They are the first and second pads of the thumbs, index, and middle fingers. **Secondary contact points** are the other four fingers. All contact points are placed toward the sides of the ball. By allowing the ball to drop into

FIGURE 5-8 Front overhead pass sequence. Courtesy of Clint Carlton.

the hands, the wrists are hyperextended (or bent backwards). The ball's force is absorbed into the first two pads of the fingers and by bringing the hands to the hair-line. The absorption portion of the pass may take from 0.03 to 0.10 second. This means there must be absorption as opposed to rebound. Once the ball is absorbed by the hands and fingers, the legs extend fully so that all body force is projected throughout the ball. The hands and arms act as two doors opening outward to project and redirect the ball. Once the ball has left the hands, the body is recoiled to its original ready position momentarily to recover from and anticipate the next play.

BACK OVERHEAD PASSING

No matter where the overhead pass is placed, the movement prior to contact should be identical so opposing players cannot anticipate the intended direction of the pass. The subtle change that occurs when executing the **back overhead pass** is a thrusting forward of the hips when ball contact is made. As a result, the body-to-ball relationship is altered enough to place the ball's trajectory backward. The quicker the hip shift, the farther the ball will be sent backward.

FIGURE 5-9 Back overhead pass sequence. Courtesy of Clint Carlton.

Checklist 4

Overhead Passing		
	YES	NO
• Movement prior to contact identical to front pass?		
• At ball contact, hips are thrust forward quickly while arms extend straight up over head by straightening the elbows?		
• Weight transferred toward target?		

The dig is used to successfully pass an opponent's attack. Its performance is similar to forearm passing recently discussed. Reading the plays accurately is important and is presented first.

READING THE DIG

READING

In order to be a successful digger on defense, the player must be able to read forming plays accurately. Reading refers to being able to evaluate and accurately anticipate where the ball will go *before* it is contacted.

While the ball is on the opponents' side of the court, a defensive player can quickly evaluate the attackers from the ready position by mentally replaying each hitter's jumping ability, preferred hand, and armswing. Once done, the ball is followed to the setter until the set direction is determined. Peripherally, the attacker's distance from the ball, the angle of approach, and wrist action should be assessed. If an adjustment in court position is necessary, it is made rapidly. As the hitter contacts the ball, focus is riveted upon the hand contacting the ball.

The synthesis of the relationship of the ball to the court, the ball to the net, and the ball to the hitter will facilitate the player's ability to read the attack. If the ball has been set close to the sideline, the line shot is not a good possibility. A set close to the net will result in a sharply hit spike. If the ball is set several feet off of the net, the blocker(s) may jump early; the ball will be hit more deeply into the court. A set diagonally passed from the back court to the front may well be a crosscourt attack. If the ball is approaching the attacker from the strong side, a likely hit would be on the angle.

Checklist 5

	YES	NO
• Have attackers been evaluated from the ready position while the ball is on the opponents' side of the court?		
• Visually follow the ball to the setter to determine set direction?		

DIGGING

The value of a defensive technique, the dig, is seldom sufficiently recognized. Without a successful dig, the setter would not have sufficient time to execute an appropriate option for the team's offensive system. The dig is the primary ingredient in converting defensive play to an attack.

Once the player has dropped to a low ready position, with the back erect, weight is forward over the balls of the feet and toward the inside of the knees. If lateral movement is necessary from the low ready position, it can be easily accomplished by dropping the knee opposite the direction of the oncoming ball to the floor. The foot that is closer to the sideline is slightly ahead of the other to keep all subsequent movement going into the court. By keeping the arms slightly flexed and in front of the body, forearms parallel with the thighs, the player can react forward or laterally quickly. As the ball is hit, the elbows slightly flexed, and the shoulder that is closer to the target is dropped. By flexing the elbows slightly, the force of the ball is cushioned and the ball will remain on your side of the net.

When attempting to read the play in anticipation of the dig, the defensive player must keep in mind two factors: the speed of the oncoming ball and the speed of the player's reactions. A ball can be hit from above the net to the endline in 0.3 to 0.7 second. A player's reaction from the moment the ball is hit to the first noticeable movements takes approximately .03 second. Therefore, it is important for the digger to be in position by the time the attacker gets to the jump phase of the spike.

The objective of using the dig in response to a high- or medium-speed attack is to get the ball into the air. With a slow-speed attack, it may be possible for the defensive player to set an overhead pass; this allows for better redirection of the ball to the setter.

It is very unlikely for the digger to be able to move into an effective position once the ball has been contacted by a hitter during a **high-speed attack.** The speed of the

Checklist 6

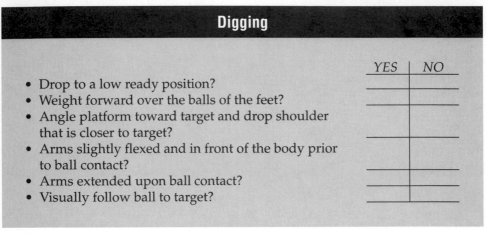

	YES	NO
Digging		
• Drop to a low ready position?		
• Weight forward over the balls of the feet?		
• Angle platform toward target and drop shoulder that is closer to target?		
• Arms slightly flexed and in front of the body prior to ball contact?		
• Arms extended upon ball contact?		
• Visually follow ball to target?		

hit is approximately 0.3 second; the player's movement time is also 0.3 second. The player must, then, be in body line *before* the hit so that the arms and hands need only be adjusted when digging. The player needs to be in a low zone of movement, stationary, and dug in by the time the attacker gets to the **foot plant,** the placing of the feet at takeoff. Visual focus is upon the hitter's hand, then to the digging action.

Usually the digger cannot move to play the hit once the attacker has contacted the ball. Because the **medium-speed attack** is slightly slower than the high-speed (0.4 to 0.7 second), it may be possible for the player to dive for the ball if it is not hit directly within the player's zone of effectiveness. The zone can be increased by four feet when using the dive.

The **slow-speed attack** (off-speed, dink) generally ranges from 0.8 to 1.4 seconds. Within this amount of time, a player can move and dig the attack even after the hitter has contacted the ball. A stationary medium zone of movement is appropriate to get the ball up if it has been read properly.

EMERGENCY MECHANICS: DIVE AND ROLL

During play, each team member must assume that the ball is coming to the zone he or she is occupying. Frequently, by narrowing focus to the hitter's eyes and then armswing, the dig position can be effectively established by the time the attacker reaches the foot plant in the spiking action. Sometimes, however, the ball is out of the defensive player's **range of effectiveness;** this range extends in a four-foot radius from the player's ready position. The dive and catch, dive and slide, and roll techniques are used to play a ball when a defensive emergency situation arises.

FIGURE 5-10 The dive and catch sequence. Photos by Susan Poag.

The primary goal of any **emergency technique** is to get the ball up and keep it in play for the team. In order to accomplish this, a defensive player must drop into a ready position in the low movement zone by flexing the knees and hips. If the ball is falling in front of the body and out of the range of effectiveness, a step forward with either foot must be taken. In the dive and catch, all of the body's weight is transferred onto the ball of the forward foot. By reaching out with both arms completely extended in front of the body in a forearm pass manner, the player can extend the range of movement even further. As the body reaches full horizontal extension, and contacts the

FIGURE 5-11 Emergency technique—the sprawl. Courtesy of D. Kluka.

Checklist 7

	YES	NO
Dive and Catch		

- Body weight transferred onto the ball of the forward foot?
- Reach out with both arms in a forearm pass manner?
- Kick the trail leg's heel up toward the ceiling?
- Push through after the ball is contacted off the forward foot?
- Arch the back upon landing?
- Absorb the force onto the chest and abdominal areas by easing the body to the floor, using the arms?

ball, the trail leg's heel is kicked up toward the ceiling. After ball contact, the player pushes through off the forward foot, placing the body in a horizontally airborne zone of movement.

Upon landing, the back is arched and the knees are flexed to absorb most of the force onto the chest and abdominal areas. To assist in the back arch, the player focuses upon the upward flight of the ball. Since the body follows the head, the arch will occur naturally if the head is tilted backward. By using the arms in a pushup manner to also absorb force, the player may also rise onto the feet again to resume play from a medium movement zone.

The dive and slide is similar to the dive and catch. It can, however, increase horizontal movement slightly farther in an emergency situation. Once in a low movement zone, a step is taken in a forward direction toward the ball. Weight is transferred onto the ball of the front foot, through the knee. By pushing forward with the lead foot, the body falls forward. The player reaches out with both arms fully extended in front of the body in a forearm pass manner. Contact with the ball is made on the forearm. Immediately after contact, the player again focuses on the upward flight of the ball. Once the ball has been contacted, the chest touches the floor; the body continues to lower and slide on the abdominal area. The arms assist in the fall by initially catching in the pushup position and pulling through. The pull-through movement is similar to that made when a person is lying on his or her stomach on a sled at the top of a hill. In order to make the sled move, the arms pull through on the sides of the body.

The **Japanese,** or **extension, roll** (so named for those who developed the technique) is an emergency technique used when a ball is outside the player's lateral

Checklist 8

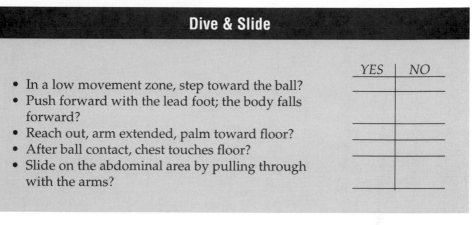

	YES	NO
Dive & Slide		
• In a low movement zone, step toward the ball?		
• Push forward with the lead foot; the body falls forward?		
• Reach out, arm extended, palm toward floor?		
• After ball contact, chest touches floor?		
• Slide on the abdominal area by pulling through with the arms?		

Checklist 9

	YES	NO
Roll		
• In a low movement zone, step laterally toward the ball?		
• Pivot on the step-out foot to turn the body in toward the target?		
• Extend the arm closer to the ball and contact it?		
• After ball contact, slide arm along floor?		
• Tuck head to the side of the extended arm?		
• Stay tucked and get to the feet quickly to continue play?		

range of effectiveness. Once in the low movement zone, a step is taken laterally toward the direction of the ball. As the body gets lower to the floor, the step-out leg flexes at the hip, knee, and ankle; the other leg remains extended. Just prior to ball contact, the step-out foot is pivoted upon; this pivoting turns the body in toward the target. The fully extended arm closer to the ball contacts it. Once it is contacted, the extended arm slides along the floor. The head is tucked to the side of the extended arm. Both knees are flexed to the chest. The knees and hips go up and over the shoulder of the nonextended arm. The player, remaining in a tucked position, is able to get to the feet quickly to continue play. Focusing upon the ball at contact

Checklist 10

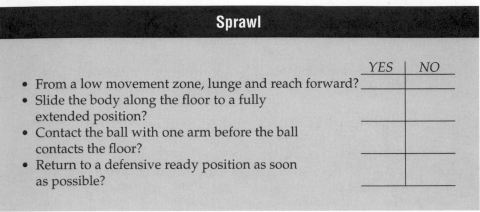

and keeping the eyes open while rolling will help the player refocus on the ball when the player has returned into a medium zone of movement.

The **sprawl** is an additional emergency technique used when a rapidly moving ball is more than a body's length in front of the player. After reaching the arms forward using a forearm passing technique, the player continues to lunge forward in a low movement zone until the body slides along the floor to a fully extended position. The ball is contacted with one arm before the ball contacts the floor.

SUMMARY

- The game of volleyball has the smallest playing surface area of any team sport. This creates two unique situations: a crowded area for movement, and a limited time to react.
- Body position should be open so the ball's position is between the body and the net. Body parts need to be stabilized at ball contact. Presentation of the appropriate surface area as soon as possible will enhance play on the ball. Ball contact should be made in body line. The player directs feet, hips, shoulders, and head/eyes toward the target area.
- Forearm passing is the key to the beginning of any team's offensive system. The body should be in a statically balanced position just prior to ball contact. To create a stable platform, the arms are extended from the shoulders and in front of the body. The ball will rebound at the angle from which it is hit, but in the opposite vertical and/or horizontal direction. If the passing platform is horizontal, the ball will rebound straight up in the air.
- The overhead pass is generally used to redirect the ball with the most accuracy offered by any skill. Coming to a stationary position before the ball arrives

assists in providing stability and time to assess the situation. For greatest accuracy, the ball should be contacted when the hands are at an angle to the intended target.

- The ball's force is absorbed into the first two pads of the fingers and by bringing the hands to the hairline. Once the ball is absorbed by the hands and fingers, the legs extend fully so that all body force is projected throughout the ball.
- The back overhead pass involves a thrusting of the hips forward when ball contact is made. As a result, the body-to-ball relationship is altered enough to place the ball's trajectory backward. The quicker the hip shift, the farther the ball will be sent backward.
- The synthesis of the relationship of the ball to the court, the ball to the net, and the ball to the hitter will facilitate the player's ability to read the attack.
- Without a successful dig, the setter would not have sufficient time to execute an appropriate option for the team's offensive system. Once the player has dropped to a low ready position, with the back erect, weight is forward over the balls of the feet and toward the inside of the knees. By keeping the arms slightly flexed and in front of the body, forearms parallel with the thighs, the player can react forward or laterally quickly. As the ball is hit, the elbows are slightly flexed, and the shoulder that is closer to the target is dropped.
- Sometimes, an emergency technique must be employed to get the ball up and keep it in play. If the ball is falling in front of the body and out of the range of effectiveness, a step forward with either foot must be taken. A dive and catch, a dive and slide, or a sprawl can be used safely. If the ball is outside the player's lateral range of effectivenes, the extension roll can be used.

▶ **assertive movement   p. 82**
moving with confidence to the ball or into position to play the ball

▶ **supportive movement   p. 82**
movement by players who are not directly involved in playing the ball

▶ **movement zones   p. 82**
levels of movement; i.e., airborne, high, medium, low

▶ **ready position   p. 82**
a position from which a variety of body movement possibilities can be executed quickly

▶ **forward movement   p. 83**
movement toward the ball in a forward direction

▶ **lateral movement   p. 84**
movement to the side to keep the midline of the body directly behind the ball when contacted

▶ **body line   p. 85**
the ball should be contacted in this line; its position would divide the player's body so that half would appear to the right of it and half to the left

▶ **balancing the court   p. 85**
zones between players are divided by size of available space and according to the weakness within the zone

▶ **seam   p. 85**
an area where there is weakness or no coverage

▶ **overset** p. 90
setting the ball to the opponents' side of the net

▶ **primary points of contact** p. 90
those points on the hands that provide power for a set

▶ **secondary points of contact** p. 90
those points on the hands that provide guidance for a set

▶ **foot plant** p. 94
placing of the feet at takeoff during an attack

▶ **high-speed attack** p. 93
speed of the hit is about 0.3 s

▶ **medium-speed attack** p. 94
speed of the hit is between 0.4 to 0.7 s

▶ **slow-speed attack** p. 94
speed of the hit is between 0.8 and 1.4 s

▶ **range of effectiveness** p. 94
a four-foot radius extending from the player's ready position

▶ **emergency technique** p. 95
a skill used to get the ball up and keep it in play for the team

Assessment 5-1

Name   Section   Date

1. Continuous Passing to Self.

   Equipment: One ball; one court; imaginary circle with radius of five feet.

   Description: Toss a volleyball to yourself; use forearm passes to continuously pass the ball to yourself. Pass the ball to a height even with the top of the net. Stay within a circle with a radius of five feet.

   Goal: 25 consecutive passes to self.

   Your performance: _____.

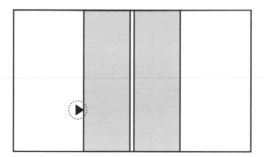

2. Forearm Pass Accuracy.

   Equipment: Ten balls; one court; one partner; target that is 10′ × 10′ between centerline, attackline, and sideline.

   Description: Partner stands behind the attack line of the opponent's court. You stand in the CB position, 1 m in the front of the endline. Partner tosses a ball over the net into the LB area of the court. You move to pass the ball to the target. Partner tosses ball to RB area.

   Goal: Twenty-five out of thirty-five you move to pass the ball to the target. Continue the process. Passes to the target, with a passing height trajectory of ten feet.

   Your performance: _____.

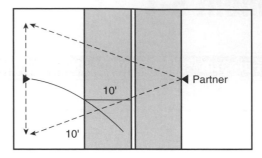

3. Move and Toss.

Equipment: Ten balls; two tossers; one receiver (you); one setter as a target.

Description: Switching between the RB and LB positions the receiver passes tosses from two tossers, both positioned in front of the attack line. They alternate tosses to you as you pass each ball to the setter who serves as a target.

Goal: Twenty of twenty-five to the target within two steps.

Your performance: _____.

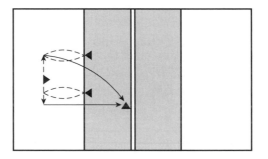

Assessment 5-2

Name   Section   Date

1. Setting Challenge.

   Equipment: Basketball hoops; one ball for two players.

   Description: One player stands at either the free throw line or top of the key. Toss the ball to yourself, and set the ball to the basket. If the ball goes in, it counts for one point if it was taken from the free throw line. It counts two points if taken from the top of the key. If the ball goes off the basket on the backboard, play continues as each player alternates attempting to score using an overhead pass. If a player's set misses the basket/backboard completely, the partner can play or start the next series from the free throw line or top of the key.

   Goal: The first to score twenty-five points wins.

   Your performance (two out of three games): _____.

2. Two Choices.

   Equipment: Two balls for every three players.

   Description: Two target-tossers are positioned, one at each side of the court. The passes begins in the MB position. The tossers alternate tosses to move the passer laterally. The tossers must overhead pass the ball back to the tosser, diagonally across from where the toss came from.

   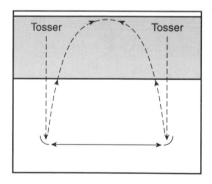

   Goal: Pass twenty of twenty-five balls to the appropriate target.

   Your performance: _____.

Assessment 5-3

Name   Section   Date

1. Pepper

   Equipment: One ball; one partner.

   Description: One player tosses the ball to the other in a downward trajectory. The second player digs the ball back to player one who sets the ball back to the second player. The second player spikes the ball back to the first player. This action continues.

   Goal: Ten digs in a sequence: hit, dig, set, hit, dig, set, etc.

   Your performance: _____.

2. Dig the Middle, Dig the Left, Dig the Right.

   Equipment: Partner, standing with the balls at the net from right side of court; several balls.

   Description: In the MB position, partner spikes the ball in an area just in front of you. You must dig the ball so that its trajectory is three feet above the net and in zone 5 (where the setter would be located). Perform the experiences from the LB position and the RB position.

   Goal: Seven out of ten in each position.

   Your performance at MB _____; at LB _____; at RB _____.

3. Perform #2 when the partner is in the middle and left areas of the court at the net.

CHAPTER 6

PUTTING THE **BALL INTO PLAY:** SERVING

OBJECTIVES

After reading this chapter, you should be able to do the following:

- Perform a variety of basic serves including the underhand floater, overhand floater, and overhand topspin.
- Describe the basic components of the various serves.
- Develop a serving strategy for game situations.

KEY TERMS

While reading this chapter, you will become familiar with the following terms:

▶ underhand floater serve
▶ overhand floater serve

▶ overhand topspin serve
▶ serving strategy

The serve is the skill used to put the ball into play; it must go over the net and into the opponents' court. Additionally, it can be used to cause a serve reception error or create an ace (a serve that leads directly to a point for the serving team). The serve is the only technique used in the game over which the player has complete control because it is begun by the player holding the ball.

There are many different types of serves used in volleyball. Each player should possess at least two different types of serves in order to facilitate the team's offensive repertoire. The underhand floater, the overhand floater, the overhand topspin, and the jump serve are the ones most frequently used in today's game. The success of any serve depends upon placement as well as power.

GENERAL SERVING CONCEPTS

- A similar serving motion pattern should be used. Dramatic or subtle changes may give the opposing team advance information and/or create inconsistencies in the serve.
- A foot position that allows for a larger base of support in the direction of the movement gives added stability. Having the opposite foot from the serving arm forward provides greater front to back balance.
- A follow-through motion ensures that the center of the arc of the serving motion is at the point of impact made by the hand on the ball; therefore, the maximum force generated is transferred from the body to the ball.
- Spin on the ball is determined by where pressure has been applied to the ball. The ball tends to spin toward the side where the least pressure is applied. Examples are seen in Figure 6-1.
- Ball trajectory is determined by the height at which the ball is contacted as well as how close to the net the contact is made. Therefore, shorter players wanting to hit a flat serve must stand farther away from the net.

The **underhand floater serve** is primarily used by young players or anyone having difficulty with the range of motion involved in overhand serving. This serve is simple to put the ball into play successfully, but it provides little challenge in serve reception by the opponents.

The body, in the high movement zone, stands behind the endline. The toes, knees, hips, and shoulders face the intended direction of the ball flight. The foot opposite the hitting hand is placed ahead of the other. Body weight is maintained by the back foot; the ball is balanced on a pedestal created by the fingers and thumb of the tossing hand and is held at waist level. Weight is transferred from back to front foot prior to contact. As the ball is tossed up to eye level, the hitting arm is swung from the shoulder straight back behind the body. The ball is hit underneath with an open palm for greater control.

Eye focus throughout the contact of the serve is directly on the back of the ball. This will aid in keeping the ball's trajectory lower to the net as well as insuring appropriate contact.

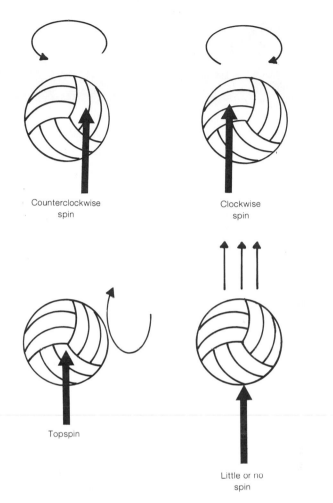

FIGURE 6-1 Where to contact the ball for various serving effects.

FIGURE 6-2 Underhand floater serve sequence. Courtesy of Clint Carlton.

Checklist 1

Underhand Floater Serve

	YES	NO
• Toes, knees, hips, and shoulders face intended direction of flight of ball?		
• Foot opposite hitting hand ahead of the other? Body weight on back foot?		
• Ball held on pedestal at waist level?		
• As ball is tossed up to eye level, hitting arm is swung straight back behind body?		
• Weight transferred from back to front foot as ball is hit underneath with open palm?		

The **overhand floater serve** is the most frequently used in the United States. Its effectiveness is a direct result of the unpredictability of its flight path. The wobbling and wiggling of the ball during flight is caused by two basic factors: the ball is compressed at contact; the greater the compression, the greater the unpredictability. The ball is hit with little or no spin. With no spin, other external forces (such as air currents) contribute to the uncertainty of its path. The ball is hit with as little contact and in as small an area as possible. The follow-through must be

FIGURE 6-3 Overhand floater serve sequence. Courtesy of Clint Carlton.

Checklist 2

Overhand Floater Serve		
	YES	*NO*
• Feet in a staggered position? Foot opposite hitting hand placed slightly ahead toes, hips, shoulders face direction ball is to travel?		
• Ball rests on a pedestal in the tossing hand at shoulder level?		
• Body weight on back foot?		
• As ball is tossed, hitting arm is cocked back, with elbow high?		
• As elbow is driven forward, weight goes to front foot?		
• At contact, heel of hand and palm contact ball through its midline; arm action stops (like punching)?		

frozen by holding the wrist rigidly upon contact. By stopping the follow-through, less force is transferred to the ball.

The body is in the high zone of movement, standing behind the endline. The feet are in a staggered position; the toes, hips, and shoulders face the direction the ball is to travel. The foot opposite the hitting hand is placed ahead of the other. The tossing arm is flexed at the elbow, with the ball resting on a pedestal made by the fingers and thumb, at shoulder level. The hitting hand is placed on the top of the ball, arm fully extended. Body weight is maintained by the back foot. The ball is tossed by lifting the arm up toward the ceiling in front of the hitting shoulder and placing the ball approximately one and one-half feet above the tossing hand. As the toss occurs, the lifting hand remains in contact with the ball as long as is comfortable. The hitting arm is cocked back by flexing the elbow and retracting the shoulder, keeping the elbow high. At the height of the toss, the weight is transferred from the back to the front foot. While the weight is transferred, the elbow is brought forward and the hand is driven to the ball. At contact, the ball is hit with the heel and palm of the hand, using a small surface area. The wrist is rigid, and the ball is hit through its midline; the arm is fully extended. As contact is made, arm action ceases. It resembles a throwing action with no follow-through.

Just prior to the serve, the player should scan the opponents' court, noticing holes in the serve reception formation or locating seams in the passing zones. Once an area is selected to serve to, focus is reverted to the ball throughout the toss, at contact, and in flight. After the ball has been given impetus, the server continues to scan the court to gain information about the developing play.

The **overhand topspin serve** travels in a predictable path and drops quickly. The topspin imparted to the ball at contact holds the ball on its course.

To begin the serve, the initial position is the same as for the floater serve. The toss of the ball, however, is approximately one and one-half feet higher. At contact, the ball is hit with the palm of the hand, and the fingers are spread and wrap over the top of the ball by flexing the wrist quickly. Because of the hand action at contact, topspin is imparted. The hitting arm is allowed to follow through completely; all movement made in the act of serving is back to front; lateral movement should be avoided as it detracts from the power of the serve.

The serve can be considered the initial defensive technique employed by a team. After the ball has been delivered, the first opportunity the serving team has to play the ball again is defensively. The serve can, with practice, be turned into an offensive weapon, utilizing deception and unpredictability to cause serve reception errors or aces. Several thoughts should be considered when serving:

A down the line serve, one within two feet of the right sideline, usually sets up a crosscourt pass; this creates more time for the serving team to adjust and read the upcoming play. This serve is also away from the strong side attacker. It is more difficult to pass the ball to the strong side area.

A crosscourt serve, one delivered from right to left, gives the attacking team more time to effectively set up an attack.

A serve to the middle of the back court can create confusion in communication with the traditional five-player serve reception formation.

If a team has a weak-passing player, that area should be served to. When a substitution occurs, the newly entered player should receive the next serve.

FIGURE 6-4 Overhand topspin serve sequence. Courtesy of Clint Carlton.

Checklist 3

Overhand Topspin Serve		
	YES	*NO*
• Same beginning position as overhand floater?		
• Ball tossed approximately three feet above shoulders?		
• At contact, ball is hit with open hand; wrist snaps forward quickly?		
• Follow-through is completed after contact?		

The first serve during the rotation should always be over the net and in the court. It should have one hundred percent accuracy but be difficult to pass efficiently.

The second serve during the same rotation should be more difficult than the first.

The development of a **serving strategy** is also beneficial to the student of the game. Possibilities for consideration include the following:

1. Directing a serve to a player who has difficulty passing. By serving tough to this type of player, an offensive advantage can be gained.
2. Serving tough to primary hitters who are unprotected in the serve reception formation. As a front row attacker, this player can be forced to receive the tough serve, then approach to attack.
3. Serving directly at the shoulders of the MF or MB player who is receiving around the 3m line in a traditional "W" serve reception pattern. If the player is the middle hitter, serving to him or her can remove the individual from the play sequence. It can also cause confusion for the MB who becomes unsure of whether to open the lane for the RB or LB to pass the ball or step back and attempt to pass.
4. Serving down the line. This is difficult to pass accurately to the setter.
5. Serving to the RF positions. This placement can force the setter to receive the ball over the inside shoulder rather than straight ahead. It can inhibit the ability to appropriately survey and set up options for offense.

There are also strategies that encompass more critical times in a match. Critical times to get serves over the net and in the court are these:

- at the beginning of a game
- after an opponent has missed the serve; momentum has shifted to your team
- after opponents' time out; momentum is probably again with your team
- after your team has won a difficult and/or long rally
- after your teammate has missed the serve

SUMMARY

- There are many types of serves used in volleyball. The success of any serve depends upon placement as well as power.
- A similar serving motion pattern should be used. A foot position that allows for a larger base of support in the direction of the movement gives added stability. Having the opposite foot from the serving arm forward provides greater front to back balance. A follow through motion ensures that the center of the arc of the serving motion is at the point of impact made by the hand on the ball. Spin on the ball is determined by where pressure has been applied to the ball. Ball trajectory is determined by the height at which the ball is contacted as well as how close to the net the contact is made.
- The development of a serving strategy is beneficial. Serving tough, directing the serve to a player who has difficulty passing, serving directly at the shoulders of the MF or MB player in a traditional "W" pattern, serving down the line, and serving to the RF position can provide possibilities for success.

▶ **underhand floater serve   p. 108**
a serve generally used by younger players to get the ball into play, particularly when strength is an issue

▶ **overhand floater serve   p. 110**
a serve which has little or no spin that produces an unpredictable flight path

▶ **overhand topspin serve   p. 112**
a serve which has topspin at contact and holds the ball on its course

▶ **serving strategy   p. 113**
a predetermined manner of how, when, and where the ball will be served to gain an advantage

Assessment 6-1

Name _____ Section _____ Date _____

1. Progressive contacts with underhand serve
   Equipment: One ball for every two players.
   Description: Players face each other on opposite sides of the court, each standing at the 3 m lines. Serving to one another, each time a player successfully serves 3 in a row to the partner, the successful player takes a large step backwards.

   Goal: to reach the endline and serve 3 consecutively over the net and in the court .

   Your performance _____ (distance).

2. Progressive contacts with overhand floater serve. Repeat the above using this serve.

3. Progressive contacts with overhand topspin serve. Repeat the above using this serve.

4. Serving close to the net.
   Equipment: Several balls; several servers; piece of elastic at least 40 feet long; antennae; court. Description: Tie the elastic to the top of each antenna. Starting at the 3m line, practice serving overhand floater or topspin serves over the net and under the elastic. Progressively move back to the endline.

   Goal: Serve 3 serves from behind the endline.

   Your performance _____ (distance).

CHAPTER 7

AT THE NET: SPIKING AND BLOCKING

OBJECTIVES

After reading this chapter, you should be able to do the following:

- Describe the basic components of spiking and blocking.
- Perform the basic attack (spike); perform a single attack or control block.
- Determine the appropriateness of when to spike and when to block.

KEY TERMS

While reading this chapter, you will become familiar with the following terms:

- ▶ hang time
- ▶ approach and takeoff
- ▶ jump and contact
- ▶ drifting
- ▶ single, double, triple block

- ▶ attack block
- ▶ control block
- ▶ multiple blocks
- ▶ commit block
- ▶ roofing the ball

ATTACKING

The culmination of a team's attack is the **spike.** It serves as one of three methods of attack by the team to display a coordinated effort. The other two methods of attack are the dink and the off-speed attack. Both will be discussed in depth in Chapter 9. How and where the spiker contacts the ball determines the team's final total endeavor. As a result, the defensive team must react to the play rather than be in control of it.

GENERAL ATTACK CONCEPTS

- Several factors influence the flight of the ball during the attack: (1) where the ball is contacted, (2) the direction of the hitter's arm swing, and (3) the force applied to the ball through the hand.
- One objective of the attack is speed. The angle of contact on the ball by the hitting hand is as much on top of the ball as possible. The smaller the angle, the more quickly the ball will be hit toward the floor.
- In order to convert horizontal movement to vertical movement, accelerate into the jump by increasing the size of the steps as well as their speed.
- The greater the number of body parts sequentially used in the attack, the greater the amount of time available to build force. That is why the ready position, the approach, the jump, the arm swing and contact, and the follow-through are sequentially important.

If too much force is applied to the ball, it may go out of bounds. If too little force is applied, the ball may go into the net.

Jumping ability plays a fundamental role in the contact point on the ball: the higher the jump, the greater the chance to hit the ball downward. The length of time spent in the air, or **hang time,** may govern the number of options available to the hitter. The longer the hang time, the better the chances of the blockers being early, the power shot being used, or the dink being employed.

The objective of the spike is to convert horizontal movement (in the approach) to vertical movement (the takeoff and jump) in order to hit the ball for the team's attack. Several aspects of hitting are important to consider in performing the spike: the **approach and takeoff** in the high zone of movement and the **jump and contact** in the airborne zone. Once the ball has been passed to the setter and its trajectory has been established, the attacker must determine where the approach to the ball is begun in relationship to the sidelines. As the ball is approaching the setter, the hitter, standing behind the 3 m line, begins bouncing in anticipation of the set; this will enable the body to be in motion to make adjustments as necessary. Lateral adjustment can easily be made once the set's trajectory is established by taking one, two, or several steps toward or away from either sideline. The adjustment is made *before* the ball reaches the highest point in its trajectory.

The step-close (two step) approach is used to gather momentum for the jump and contact of the ball. For a left-handed player, the sequence is right-left, right.

For the right-hander, it is left-right, left. In either case, the first step is a long one directly toward the net. The close, or second step, is made with one foot planted (heel-toe) slightly before the other. The planting of one foot just before the other helps to minimize **drifting.** Drifting moves the body laterally rather than vertically at takeoff.

While bouncing, the arms remain in the ready position. The arms swing forward with the first step. During the close step, the arms are extended straight behind the body as both feet plant. The body is flexed slightly forward once both feet have contacted the floor.

As the feet are planted, the arms are thrust upward so that the nonhitting arm is pointing toward the ball; the shoulders turn when the hitting arm is cocked with the elbow up, reaching down the back with the thumb. The hitting arm is rapidly driven through the upper half of the ball. The wrist snaps forward with the palm of the hand open, fingers widespread. Upon landing on both feet, the knees and hips are flexed to absorb force. To hit the ball crosscourt, the thumb is turned down as the ball is contacted; to hit down the line, the thumb is up; to go over the block, the ball should be hit deeply by contacting it toward the center.

The visual pattern must be accomplished quickly because the spiking action takes only seconds. The first contact of the ball should be seen peripherally. The ball is then focused upon through the setter's contact. Once the direction of the set is determined, the ball continues to be focused upon. As the jump is made, the

FIGURE 7-1 The spike sequence. Courtesy of Clint Carlton.

Checklist 1

The Spike		
	YES	NO
• Laterally adjust before ball reaches its highest point?		
• Approach begun when ball is at the apex of its trajectory?		
• Use step-close approach? Arms swing forward with first step? Arms extend straight behind body as both feet plant?		
• Thrust both arms up while jumping? Hitting arm is cocked with elbow high?		
• As arm is driven through ball, wrist snaps forward with open hand?		
• Contact ball with arm at full extension?		
• Land on both feet, balls of feet first; hips and knees flex to absorb force?		

block and a primary defensive player are seen peripherally. The ball is focused upon through contact.

BLOCKING

Blocking and digging (discussed in Chapter 5) are two skills that are reactions to attacks made by the opposing team. The blocker and digger attempt to shorten their reaction times as well as improve their accuracy.

GENERAL BLOCKING CONCEPTS

- The body is put into motion by transferring momentum from one part of the body to the total body. Adjusting the body's position relative to the attacker's position is critical to blocking effectiveness. The feet should be moved first so the body is aligned appropriately with the attacker. Positioning varies from single to double to triple block.
- Beginning the block from a stationary position increases the potential for maximum vertical jumping and appropriate timing. By keeping the hands in the "Mickey Mouse Ears" position, the amount of time needed to perform the jump is lessened, thereby increasing the chances of timing the block successfully.

- When the body becomes airborne, transfer of momentum must occur at the instant of takeoff. Once the body is in the air, limited adjustments in position can be made. Frequently, reaching the hands toward the ball occurs because an adjustment had to be made after takeoff.
- Spread the fingers of the hands when contacting the ball. The greater the surface area exposed to the ball, the greater the chance for surrounding the ball and successfully blocking it.
- To help achieve the accuracy of the block, the eyes must be focused on the ball. Keep the eyes open and focused through contact.

The primary objective of the block is to become the first line of defense and seal off the net. Secondly, it is to prevent the power shot by taking away a portion of the court from the opponents. The block may be performed by one, two, or three players in the front court. Because the rules limit the act of blocking to front court players, a **single** (solo), **double,** or **triple block** can be used. The two most frequently used blocks are the single and double. Triple blocking requires great skill and coordinated team effort. It is used somewhat infrequently, as its effectiveness relative to intensity of effort and time produces diminishing returns for the blocking team. Double and triple blocks are also referred to as **multiple blocks.**

Two types of single blocks are used by most teams: an **attack block** and a **control block.** The attack block's functions are to angle the ball down onto the opponents' side of the court after it is contacted by the attacker and to score points. A control block slows the speed of the ball and rebounds it up into the air on the blockers' side of the court. The control block may be successfully used by a shorter player who has a limited vertical jump or as a specific strategy maneuver to enhance a balanced attack opportunity. An overhead pass may be used on the first ball off this block for greater control to facilitate a three-hit attack.

Many teams, when using multiple blocks, choose to **commit block,** or plan in advance to block a predetermined hitter.

The most difficult time to use a multiple block, however, is when defending against a quick attack, generally from the middle. Because the set is only a foot above the net, blockers are severely limited in their time to close the block.

Before the ball crosses the net, the potential blocker assumes the blocking ready position. The player faces the net, ten inches away from it. The feet are shoulder width apart; knees and hips are slightly flexed. The weight of the body is balanced on the balls of the feet. The hands are placed in the "Mickey Mouse Ears" position, arms flexed at the elbows, fingers even with the ears, palms of the hands parallel to the net.

FIGURE 7-2 Reaching the hands toward the ball on a double block. Courtesy of Purdue University Photographic Services.

FIGURE 7-3 Spread the fingers for greater surface area exposure.

FIGURE 7-4 Blocking ready position. Courtesy of D. Kluka.

The blocker, while the play develops, watches the pass to the setter and peripherally checks the primary hitter (the one most set to, comes through in critical situations, is on the power side, or in the middle). Focus continues through the setter's contact and moves with the ball until set direction is determined. Once done, focus is adjusted to the hitter.

From the ready position, the player adjusts by one, two, or a series of slide steps. The hitter's swing is in line with the blocker's nose. To move to the left, the player pushes off of the right foot. A large lateral step is made with the left foot, followed rapidly by the right. If necessary, additional steps can be taken again. The shoulders are kept parallel to the net. To move to the right, the procedure is reversed.

FIGURE 7-5 Two-count single block sequence. Courtesy of Clint Carlton.

Once the body is positioned appropriately, a two-count block is performed. Count one is the jump, from a squat, and reach; count two is the retraction of the arms and landing. The hands and fingers are spread to cover as much area as possible with the index fingers parallel. The arms go straight up along the face of the net and then over toward the approaching ball. The forearms are close to the net and in front of the body. Elbows are stiff, but wrists are relaxed to ball contact so

Checklist 2

Blocking		

Attack Block

	YES	NO
• Assume blocking ready position at the net?		
• Feet shoulder width apart, hands at "Mickey Mouse Ears" level?		
• Watch the opposing setter?		
• Once the set direction is known, focus on the attacker's hitting shoulder?		
• Line up with your nose even with the attacker's hitting shoulder?		
• Jump just after attacker jumps?		
• Hands spread with index fingers parallel?		
• Reach toward the ball?		
• Retract arms as you return from jump height?		
• Land on both feet, and flex hips and knees to absorb force?		

Control Block?

	YES	NO
• Save initial position of attack block?		
• Just before ball contact, angle wrists backward?		
• Arms are straight up toward ceiling?		
• Land on both feet and flex hips and knees to absorb force?		

the blocker can better react to the attacker's last-second adjustments and redirect the ball at contact. Visual focus is through the thumbs and index fingers. If the ball passes through the block, the blocker turns in the direction the ball has passed in order to attempt to play the ball again if necessary.

To become more successful at one-on-one attack blocking, the blocker should consider the following concepts:

- On sets close to the net, the ball should be covered completely, or **roofed.**
- The hands should be pulled down if the attacker attempts to dink off of the block.
- The eyes should be kept open throughout the blocking action.
- The outside hand should be turned in to the court in order to direct down-the-line hits back into the hitter's court.

- If the attacker can clearly hit over the block, a deflective block may be used effectively.

The control block is performed quite similarly to the attack block just described. Instead of reaching with the hands toward the ball, the wrists are cocked back with fingers widespread. The ball rebounds off the palms high into the air over the blocker's side of the court.

SUMMARY

- The spike serves as one of three methods of attack by the team to display a coordinated effort. Several factors influence the flight of the ball during the attack: where the ball is contacted, the direction of the hitter's arm swing, and the force applied to the ball through the hand. The angle of contact on the ball by the hitting hand is as much on top of the ball as possible. In order to convert horizontal movement to vertical movement, acceleration into the jump by increasing the size of the steps as well as their speed is necessary. The greater the number of body parts sequentially used in the attack, the greater the amount of time available to build force.
- The block is a reaction to an attack by the opposing team. Beginning the block from a stationary position increases the potential for maximum vertical jumping and appropriate timing. When the body becomes airborne, transfer of momentum must occur at the instant of takeoff. Once the body is in the air, limited adjustments in position can be made. Spread the fingers of the hands when contacting the ball. The greater the surface area exposed to the ball, the greater the chance for surrounding the ball and successfully blocking it.
- The control block is performed similarly to the attack block. The wrists, however, are cocked back with fingers widespread. The ball rebounds off the palms high into the air over the blocker's side of the court.

▶ **hang time   p. 118**
the length of time a player spends in the air when jumping

▶ **approach and takeoff   p. 118**
used in the spike and performed in the high movement zone

▶ **jump and contact   p. 118**
used in the spike and performed in the high movement zone

▶ **drifting   p. 119**
the act of moving the body laterally rather than vertically at takeoff in spiking

▶ **single, double, triple block   p. 121**
the team's first line of offense, using one, two, or three players to confront the ball after it has been attacked

▶ **attack block   p. 121**
a block used to angle the ball down onto the opponents' side of the court after it is contacted by the attacker and to score points

▶ **control block   p. 121**
a block generally used by a shorter player who has a limited vertical jump

or a specific strategy maneuver to enhance a balanced attack opportunity

▶ **multiple blocks**   **p. 121**
blocks that include two or three teammates; double or triple blocks

▶ **commit block**   **p. 121**
plan in advance to block a predetermined hitter

▶ **roofing the ball**   **p. 123**
on sets close to the net, the ball is covered completely by the blocker

Assessment 7-1

_____   _____   _____
Name   Section   Date

1. Spiking against the wall.

   Equipment: ball; wall with no obstructions.

   Description: Stand facing a wall, 10 feet away. Spike the ball to the floor so that it bounces before it hits the wall. The ball will rebound off the floor and into the wall. As the ball returns, adjust and spike the ball again.

   Goal: Twenty-five consecutive spikes.

   Your performance: _____ (consecutive hits).

2. Approach, hit, and direct.

   Equipment: partner; several balls; cones; court.

   Description: Mark two areas that are 10′ × 10′ in the LB and RB areas with cones. Your partner serves as a setter. Pass the ball high to your partner. The partner sets back to you, the hitter. From the LF position, spike the ball to one of the two areas marked on the opposing side of the court.

   Goal: Six out of ten in the LB area; six out of ten in the RB area.

   Your performance: _____ LB; _____ RB.

3. Approach, hit and direct from a back zone, pass markings from #2 on the court.

   Equipment: court; several balls; two partners.

   Description: The ball is tossed from the MB area to the setter; the setter sets the ball to the hitter; the hitter spikes the ball to the LB or RB position.

   Goal: Seven out of ten in the LB area; seven out of ten in the RB area.

   Your performance: _____ LB; _____ RB.

Assessment 7-2

Name   Section   Date

1. Toss and Block.

   Equipment: Partner as a tosser on one side of the net; court; several balls.

   Description: Partner tosses the ball, using a two-handed overhead throw and jumps over the net. As the blocker, you jump to block the ball before it comes over the net. The block should land in the opponent's court.

   Goal: Seven out of ten blocks.

   Your performance: _____.

2. Continuous Blocking.

   Equipment: Six players; court.

   Description: Six players assume blocking positions, three on one side of the net, three on the other. Each player begins by jumping and blocking in place. All players move one position to the right and synchronize their blocks so that they attempt to touch hands above the net.

   Goal: Block in all positions five times each, touching the hands above the net without contacting the net.

   Your performance: _____.

3. Spiker Awareness.

   Equipment: Four players; cart of balls; court.
   Description: Player one (spiker) is positioned on the opposite side of the net from player two (blocker). The tosser tosses a ball from behind the blocker to the spiker, who approaches and spikes. The blocker watches the attacker to get cues needed to block the ball. The attacker then moves back off the net to attack again.

   Goal: Ten experiences.

   Your performance: What five cues did you attend to?

CHAPTER 8

INTRODUCTORY PLAYING SYSTEMS:

OFFENSE

AND DEFENSE

OBJECTIVES

After reading this chapter, you should be able to do the following:

- Describe the importance of passing accuracy as it relates to basic serve reception.
- Understand the basic 4–2 offensive system, its serve reception pattern, its attack coverage, and its free ball situations.
- Understand basic defense and the 2–1–3 system of playing defense.
- Experience basic offensive and defensive systems.

KEY TERMS

While reading this chapter, you will become familiar with the following terms:

▶ primary target area

▶ opening passing lanes

▶ "W" pattern

▶ 4–2 offensive system

▶ attack coverage

▶ free ball situations

Continued on p. 132.

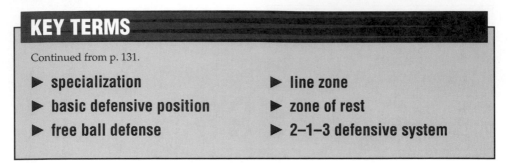

KEY TERMS

Continued from p. 131.

- ▶ specialization
- ▶ basic defensive position
- ▶ free ball defense

- ▶ line zone
- ▶ zone of rest
- ▶ 2–1–3 defensive system

Passing accuracy is vital to offensive success. The quality of the initial pass of the serve to the setter is important. Because of the types of serves used in today's game as well as rule interpretations, a forearm pass is generally used to play the ball. Basic serve reception is Number One in systems play for any team.

This pass needs to give the setter enough time to get to the ball; the ball should have little spin and force. If the ball is effectively passed to the **primary target area** (the area on the net between the middle front and the right front positions), any team playing any type of offensive system (4–2, 5–1, 6–2) can smoothly initiate its selected attack.

In order to sustain effective communication during serve reception, assertive movement toward an approaching ball is vital. "Mine," or, "I've got it" is an appropriate response to teammates. During service reception, **opening the passing lanes** is critical for the success of the first pass. As the served ball travels toward the net, the potential passers face the server. As the ball passes over the net, all players not directly involved with the pass pivot and open toward the passer (supportive movement). At contact, all players focus upon the ball, and their feet, hips, and shoulders are open to the ball so that each has the opportunity to play it in body line. Back court players always have priority if they have a better opportunity to play the ball in body line.

If the ball is at chest height or above, they let the ball go, as it will be out. They will call the ball out when close to the sidelines for front row players. They will move more assertively to take a ball that is served to the deep middle of the court when they play the LB position.

Front row players allow balls that are chest high or above to be played by back row players. They move forward to play balls that are short, but seldom move backward to receive a ball.

FIGURE 8-1 Players have opened the passing lane. Courtesy of the University of Central Oklahoma Photographic Services.

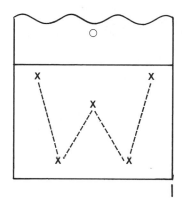

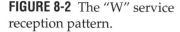

O = not involved in reception pattern
X = potential service receivers

FIGURE 8-2 The "W" service reception pattern.

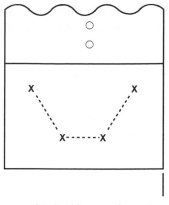

O = not involved in reception pattern
X = potential service receivers

FIGURE 8-3 The "U" service reception pattern.

Setters never receive the serve, always call serves that are short, call for the pass, and raise the hand closer to the net as a target for the first pass. They also position themselves when setting to face the left sideline with the right foot forward as the pass approaches.

Generally, two types of service reception patterns are used—a "W" or 5-player pattern and a "U" or 4-player pattern. Each pattern is named after the letter of the alphabet it resembles. The most commonly used pattern is the "**W pattern.**" The "W" can be used effectively with an offense utilizing 3 attackers as well as the 4–2.

The "U" pattern for service reception involves only 4 players. It can be used effectively with any offensive system (4–2, 6–2, 5–1). It allows more time for the middle attacker to establish position for the quick set. By making minor adjustments in positioning (shifting), the setter has more time to reach the primary target area at the moment of service.

If a player is unsuccessful in passing the service, the "U" pattern can be adjusted to eliminate him or her from the reception pattern. The short serve to the center of the court, however, makes this pattern a poor choice if the team does not pass well.

The actual designation of which player fulfills which position on the court will, of course, vary depending upon the offensive system used and where setters are in the rotation.

OFFENSIVE SYSTEMS

Selection of an effective offensive system requires a knowledge of each system's strategy and a realistic assessment of a team's abilities and limitations. The rules prohibit any player overlapping another player at the moment of service. Because of this, offensive systems and serve reception patterns appear intricate and detailed. The main objective of each rotation (one position, clockwise), in any system is to gain a strategic advantage: get the setter to the appropriate area of the court quickly in order to execute the attack. Several systems are available for selection by a volleyball team: 4–2, International, 4–2, 6–2, and 5–1 are frequently used.

4–2 OFFENSIVE SYSTEM (FRONT COURT SETTER SYSTEM)

The **4–2 offensive system** is generally the first system learned by a team. It contains the most simple, straightforward offense. The setter is a front row player; therefore, the team only has two attackers. The two setters are placed opposite one another in the rotational order; one setter is always located in the front row. The other four players are primarily attackers, making hitting responsibilities easier. Once the ball is served, the front row setter moves or switches into the center of the front court close to the net. The remaining players in the front court, the attackers, become outside hitters.

Using this system, there is less total movement within the team; therefore, a team with moderate skill may incorporate the system effectively. The attack is limited to the right and left sides of the court, thereby creating more down-the-line or crosscourt shots. The best hitter is placed on the left; the better setter is placed behind the best hitter so that both can remain in the front court for more rotations.

In the 4–2 system, the setters are initially placed in the CF and CB positions. The setter, while in the front zone, is responsible for all primary setting. The primary

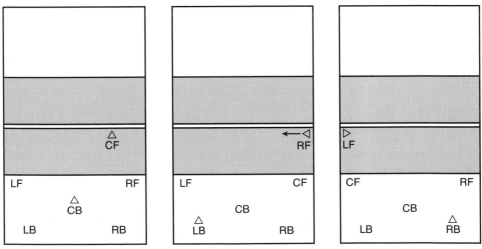

△ = setters

FIGURE 8-4 Serve reception for 4–2 offensive system using a W-formation.

setter is hidden in the front zone so that the player is not involved in receiving the serve. When the setter is in the RF or LF positions, a switch must occur at serve contact. Upon contact on the serve, the primary setter then moves into the CF positions and has two options for the offensive plays—front set and back set. When the setter is in the CF position, no switching needs to occur.

ATTACK COVERAGE

Once the serve has been received, the ball is passed to begin an offensive play. As the play develops, the opposing team adjusts its defense for **attack coverage.** It is imperative that the offense covers the attacker and the court. There are basically five results that complete an offensive play:

1. the attacker pummels the ball to the floor;
2. the attacker hits the ball out-of-bounds or into the net, making an error;
3. the blocker blocks the ball, and it goes out-of-bounds or the blocker makes an error;
4. the defense digs the ball and it remains in play;
5. the blocker blocks the ball and it remains in play; or
6. the blocker blocks the ball successfully for sideout or point.

If the ball remains in play, it is vital for the offensive team to be in position, just prior to the attacker's contact with the ball. To effectively cover the court, a 3–2 attack coverage is frequently used. This means that 3 players form a semicircle behind the attacker; the other two split the area behind and between those in the semicircle.

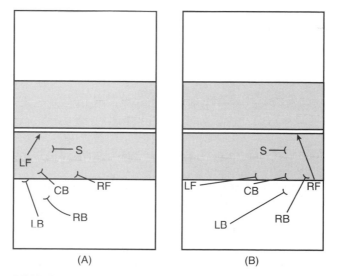

(A)   (B)

FIGURE 8-5 (A) Attack coverage when LF is the attacker. (B) Attack coverage when RF is the attacker.

The setter is always the one closest to the net. The center back is always in the center of the semicircle. The back closest to either sideline (LB or RB) completes the semicircle. The others simply fill in the spaces for support.

FREE BALL SITUATIONS

Sometimes an anticipated attack becomes a broken play, where the team cannot control the ball well enough to complete an attack. Perhaps the ball is not initially passed well; the setter is then unable to place the ball well enough for the hitter to give the ball a downward trajectory. This situation presents a **free ball situation.**

A free ball situation provides a team with the opportunity to move from a basic defense

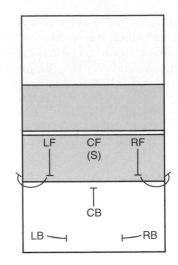

FIGURE 8-6 From basic defense to free ball position.

position to a basic W-formation for an attack. The LF and RF back up and assume hitting positions, while back row players adjust to basic offensive positions.

BASIC DEFENSIVE SYSTEMS

The major objective of attack coverage is to keep the ball in play, if the block beats the attack. It is the attacker's responsibility to beat the block if possible. Defensive players, however, must react; attacking players can make things happen.

Several defensive concepts are necessary for every player to understand:

- In all defensive systems, each player's responsibility is to beat the hitter to the foot plant. This forces the defensive player to become stationary before digging the ball.
- All players must know who is responsible for the dink.
- If there is a no-block situation, potential blockers must move off the net and pass.
- The middle back player must be able to reach the ball within a large zone of responsibility.
- **Specialization** of back court players is beneficial to assist in communication about zones of responsibility (right back, usually a setter; middle back, usually the quickest defensive player; left back, usually good reaction time).

All defensive systems (player-up, player-back, etc.) are designed to develop an effective block, maximize court coverage, and limit the opponents' attack choices. While a team is waiting for the opponents' offensive play to develop, a **basic defensive position** is established. From this basic transition defensive position, all other defenses can be easily and smoothly achieved.

The three front court players anticipate the attack in the blocking ready position to form any double block combination necessary. The back court players assume positions that will permit movement only into the court. As the play is read, adjustments are made rapidly by moving up, back, or laterally.

If the flight of the ball has a high trajectory, a **free ball defense** is easily implemented. Players call "free," and the setter rapidly reverts to the appropriate area near the net so that the second team contact is made there. All other players assume areas on the court used for service reception, being certain to focus upon and face the ball. The first contact may be made easily with an overhand pass.

The defensive court can be divided into several areas of coverage. The individual player responsible for a particular zone may change depending upon the system used by the team. Zone 1 is known as the power zone (Fig. 8-7). If the ball gets through the block, it will have its greatest speed. Zone 2 is the **off-block zone**. Cut shots and inside dinks generally frequent this area. Zone 5 is called the **line zone.** In this zone, there is very little time for the digger to react if the ball gets past the block. Zone 6 is referred to as the **zone of rest.** If the ball enters the deep area of the court, the player has the most time to react (but that time is in milliseconds). Understanding these basic zones assists the defensive player in determining zones of effectiveness for each specific defensive system.

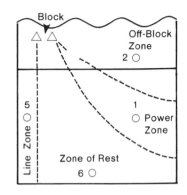

FIGURE 8-7 Zones of defensive coverage.

2–1–3 DEFENSE SYSTEM

When the opposing team generates an attack, a suitable defense includes a block and court coverage. A standard type of defense is a 2–1–3. This defense represents two blockers, one player behind the block, and three backcourt players. The assumption inherent in the system is that the block will take away the need for defending the backcourt directly behind it. The player positioned behind the block is ready to pick up any attack that is off-speed, including a dink. Each defensive player is basically responsible for either a hard attack or an off-speed shot, which lessens the likelihood of surprise.

The basic **2–1–3 defense** is fairly simple to execute. The CB stage in the middle of the court. The

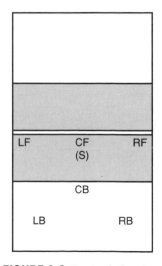

FIGURE 8-8 Basic defensive position for 2–1–3 defense.

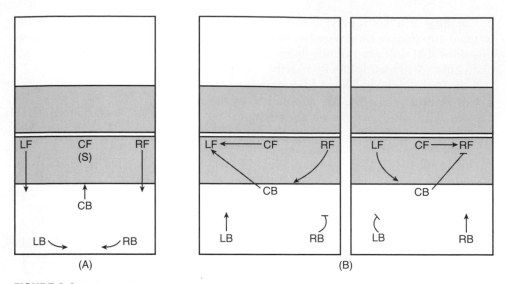

FIGURE 8-9 (A) Free ball position from basic defense (2–1–3). (B) Block coverage, using a 2–1–3 defense.

attackers and setter remain near the net, ready to block. The other two back row players (LB and RB) remain in the back one-third of the court, near each sideline.

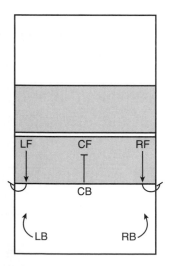

FIGURE 8-10 Block coverage for a middle attack, using a 2–1–3 defense.

This basic defensive position is maintained until the setter indicates the need to move to a free ball positions.

If a block is imminent, the middle blocker moves to the side where the attack is forming. The outside blocker sets the block, the middle closes to the outside, and the remaining players assume their positions just before the attacker gets to the jump in the attack. The outside blocker focuses on the ball, while the middle blocker concentrate on the angle shot.

If the attack comes from the center, it is usually a quick attack. A single block is used. Both off-blockers back up to the 3 m line, while the CB moves forward and the LB and RB swing to the sidelines to pick up the angle attack.

SUMMARY

- Passing accuracy is vital to offensive success. Basic serve reception is Number One in systems play for any team. The "W" or "U" pattern of serve reception has been proved effective.
- The 4–2 system is generally the first system learned by a team. It contains the most simple, straight-forward offense. The setter is a front row player; therefore, the team only has two attackers in each rotation.
- There are five results that complete any offensive play: the attacker pummels the ball to the floor; the attacker hits the ball out of bounds or into the net; the blocker blocks the ball, and it goes out of bounds or the blocker makes an error; the defense digs the ball and it remains in play; the blocker blocks the ball and it remains in play; or the blocker blocks the ball successfully for sideout or point.
- The major objective of attack coverage is to keep the ball in play, if the block beats the attack. Defensive players, however, must react. Attacking players can make things happen.
- When the opposing team generates an attack, a suitable defense includes a block and block and court coverage. A standard type of defense is a 2–1–3. This defense represents two blockers, one player behind the block, and three backcourt players. In this system, the block will take away the need for defending the backcourt directly behind it.

▶ **primary target area   p. 132**
area on the net between the middle front and the right front positions

▶ **opening passing lanes   p. 132**
as the ball passes over the net, all players not directly involved with the pass pivot and open toward the passer

▶ **"W" pattern   p. 133**
a pattern for service reception involving 5 players, shaped in a "W"

▶ **4–2 offensive system   p. 134**
two setters are placed opposite one another in the rotational order; the other four players are attackers

▶ **attack coverage   p. 135**
as play develops, the opposing team adjusts its defense to defend the ensuing attack by covering the attacker and the court

▶ **free ball situations   p. 136**
when a play must be converted to a high, slow ball traveling over the net

▶ **specialization   p. 136**
players have particular responsibilities, e.g., right back, usually a setter; middle back, usually the quickest defensive player; left back, usually good reaction time

▶ **basic defensive position** p. 136
a team's basic position as play develops on the other side of the court

▶ **free ball defense** p. 137
setter rapidly reverts to the appropriate area near the net so that the second team contact is made

▶ **line zone** p. 137
Zone 5, with little time to react defensively

▶ **zone of rest** p. 137
Zone 6, with the ball entering the deep area of the court defensively

▶ **2–1–3 defensive system** p. 137
two blockers, one player behind the block, and three back court players

Assessment 8-1

Name _____   Section _____   Date _____

1. Serve, Pass, and Set.

   Equipment: Court; 5 players; cart of balls

   Description: Player 1 serves to Player 2. Player 2 passes the ball to the setter (Player 3). The setter sets the ball to Player 4. Player 4 catches the ball and rolls the ball back to Player 5. Player 5 gives a new ball to Player 6. Players rotate from server to receiver, receiver to setter, setter to catcher, catcher to shagger, and shagger to server.

   Goal: Complete seven out of ten passes to the setter.

   Your performance: _____.

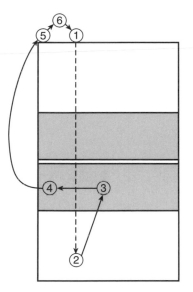

2. Pass, Set, Attack, Cover.

   Equipment: Tosser.

   Description: Tosser serves to Player 1. Player 1 passes to the setter. The setter sets high to Player 2. Player 1 and the setter move to cover Player 2. Player 2 spikes the ball, gets the ball, and goes to the end of the shagging line. Others rotate by following the flight of the ball.

Goal: Get through the sequence successfully six of ten times.

Your performance: _____.

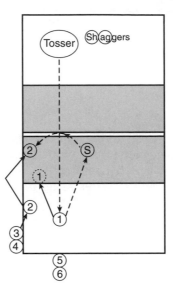

Assessment 8-2

Name   Section   Date

FRONT ZONE PLAYERS

	Yes	No
• Hands in Mickey Mouse ears position?		
• Move along net to left or right?		
• Little or no arm swing when jumping?		
• Reach for the ball?		
• If the off-blocker, back pedal to 3 m line for defense?		

BACK ZONE PLAYERS

	Yes	No
• Body in low movement zone?		
• Weight forward?		
• Focus on ball?		

CHAPTER 9

ADVANCED SKILLS

OBJECTIVES

After reading this chapter, you should be able to do the following:

- Describe the basic components of the jump serve, jump set, setter attack, back row attack, back slide attack, quick attack, and multiple block (double).
- Experience the jump serve, jump set, setter attack, back row attack, back slide attack, quick attack, and multiple block.
- Understand the strategic use of each of these skills.

KEY TERMS

While reading this chapter, you will become familiar with the following terms:

► **jump serve**

► **jump set**

► **setter attack**

► **dink (tip)**

► **quick attack**

► **back row attack**

Continued on p. 146.

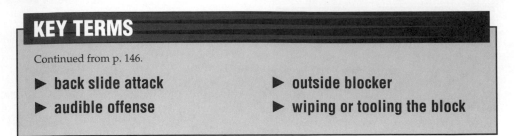

KEY TERMS

Continued from p. 146.

▶ **back slide attack**

▶ **audible offense**

▶ **outside blocker**

▶ **wiping or tooling the block**

Once the basics of passing, serving, attacking, and blocking have been established in the volleyball player's repertoire, a series of advanced skills can be undertaken to make the game more interesting and exciting. Techniques of the jump serve, various overhead passes such as the jump set and setter attack, off-speed attacks, slide attack, back row attacks, and multiple blocks are included.

JUMP SERVE

The most sophisticated and complex serve is the **jump serve.** It was originally developed for the men's game. The height of the net in the men's game creates a different trajectory with most traditional serves. A different type of serve was needed as an offensive weapon—the jump serve seemed to be the answer. It found its way into the women's game as well. In the 1985 NCAA Women's National Championships, it was first effectively used.

Checklist 1

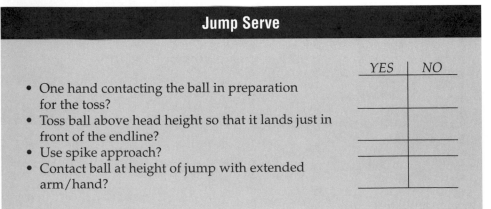

Jump Serve

	YES	NO
• One hand contacting the ball in preparation for the toss?		
• Toss ball above head height so that it lands just in front of the endline?		
• Use spike approach?		
• Contact ball at height of jump with extended arm/hand?		

FIGURE 9-1 Jump serve sequence. Courtesy of Clint Carlton.

It has been estimated that Karch Kiraly was clocked at performing a **jump serve** over 23 m/s or 52 mph. As a result, jump serve as an advanced skill can provide additional variety for offense. The server can produce extraordinary velocities to the ball at the onset of each rally. Using traditional serving techniques during the 1996 Olympic Games, such as a topspin, serves averaged 33 mph. It is obvious that with nearly a 20 mph difference, the jump serve can be used to provide the defense with far less time to react. With limited time for serve reception, the attack which ultimately rebounds may be far less than optimal.

The jump serve also provides a lower trajectory of delivery by approximately 6 degrees when compared with topspin or floater serves. During serve reception, the player must provide a platform that has an increased angle, thereby causing the passed ball to fly in a higher trajectory. The higher trajectory can cause the ball to reach the setter at a reduced speed, thereby altering the timing of the attack.

Using the jump serve can also strategically place the server onto the court in a more ready position. Sometimes in traditional serving, the server is left outside the court, observing the results of the serve. The observation of the serve might be long enough to alter the player's defensive positioning.

Although the jump serve has advantages, it is also not without disadvantages. For example, the accuracy of the serve is less than those of traditional serves. Even at the international level, there seems to be a slight deviation in success rates between the jump and other serves. The timing of the toss, along with the timing of the jump and ball contact, is critical to the efficiency and effectiveness.

It would be interesting to see what would happen if this skill was added to the basic skills list. Perhaps it might be that its accuracy, its timing, and its jump would become part and parcel of those skills which are necessary for volleyball success.

THE TOSS

A consistent toss is critical to the success of this serve. It should be performed with one hand so that forces are placed on the ball only in the direction the ball is intended to travel. Using the hitting hand to toss the ball can provide the player with more control. Using the non-hitting hand to toss the ball uses the notion of skills transfer consistently. The toss must be made toward the endline. Players should experiment with both and use the one that is more comfortable. Its peak trajectory should be reached approximately one to three feet behind the endline.

APPROACH

So that as much of the opponents' court can be used, the approach should be made almost perpendicular to the court. The approach resembles a right-left-right close and jump rhythm if the player is right-handed. Two short steps, followed by a long step to a jump close completes the footwork. The armswing on the approach to the jump serve should resemble the preparatory phase of the armswing when the ball is hit for an attack. By adding the power of the jump and the armswing, this momentum increases the velocity of the ball.

CONTACT

Ball contact should happen when the server is at the peak portion of the jump. Once the ball is contacted, the arm follows through completely.

In general, two factors contribute to the success of serving any ball. First, the palm should face toward the target. Second, by looking down the arm at contact, the ball should appear to fly in a trajectory in line with the arm.

VARYING OVERHEAD PASSES

JUMP SET

The **jump set,** when used in combination with a quick middle attack, can be the fastest play in the game of volleyball. The use of the jump set reduces the time it takes for the ball to get from the setter to the quick attack hitter. The jump set was originally designed to force the middle blocker to commit to the middle attack. The setter has the option of setting a shoot to the outside to create a one-on-one situation for the outside hitter.

The jump set closely resembles an overhead pass executed from the floor. As the pass approaches, the knees are flexed, with the right foot ahead of the left. The setter uses a step-close takeoff, stepping right and closing left. The right foot plant is beneficial in avoiding drifting, the shifting of the body laterally during takeoff. By planting the foot closer to the net first, the drift can be minimized, thereby avoiding a net foul.

FIGURE 9-2 A jump set is used for a quick middle attack. Courtesy of USA Volleyball.

Checklist 2

Jump Set Sequence		
	YES	NO
• Flex knees?		
• Step right, close left and jump?		
• Contact ball just above the forehead?		

FIGURE 9-3 Jump set sequence. Courtesy of Clint Carlton.

Once in the airborne movement zone, the hands are brought into the setting position. Ball contact is made just above the forehead with the hands open, arms in the normal setting position. Shoulders are perpendicular to the net. The arms are extended fully to assist with placement and power. As the pass approaches from the back court, all hitters are in peripheral vision. Primary focus is concentrated upon the ball. As the setter jumps, the blocker's movements are also seen peripherally. The information gathered from the hitters and blocker will assist in the determination of the type of set that will be delivered from the jump set.

Jump setting can also be accomplished as a back pass. The back is arched as the ball is contacted at the height of the jump. By contacting the ball in the same position relative to the head, the jump back set is quite deceiving to any defensive player and creates greater variety for the team's attack options.

SETTER ATTACK

As a setter, attacking (tipping) the ball over the net on the second contact after deceiving the opponents with a preliminary setting motion can be effective. It can occur in conjunction with a jump set. The hands are in the setting position. As the ball's trajectory travels over the left shoulder, the palm of the left hand faces the net. Contact with the ball is made on its upper side by the pads of the fingers. If the ball is contacted by the left hand at the bottom, the ball will be directed too long to constitute a legal contact. A left-handed setter has great versatility with this skill. Timing and the contact of the ball by a quick snap of the wrist in the desired direction the ball is to go should make the shot effective. The visual focus needs to be kept upon the ball through contact. Allowing the eyes to scan or refocus on the

FIGURE 9-4 Setter attack sequence. Courtesy of Clint Carlton.

attacker or defender(s) could give away the element of surprise when using the **setter attack.**

The setter attack can be successfully used when a back court defensive player is deep in the court. The ball should be placed in front of the back court player to force the player to use an emergency technique to play the ball. The primary area of the court in which to place the ball is immediately behind the 3 m line, because blockers will then be generally ineffective in getting to the ball successfully.

VARYING ATTACKS

OFF-SPEED

The off-speed attack is similar to a change-up pitch in softball or baseball. Defensive players generally settle in to defending a certain pattern of attack—pass, set, high-speed hit. The defense usually keys on the hitter's armswing. By slowing the speed of the armswing and snapping the wrist in a specific direction, the defensive team can be caught off balance.

FIGURE 9-5 An off-speed attack is designed to go around the block. Courtesy of USA Volleyball.

Checklist 3

Dink/Tip Attack		
	YES	*NO*
• Use same pattern as a spike?		
• At the last moment, reduce the speed of the hitting arm and contact the ball with fingers widespread?		
• "Place" the ball over the blockers' hands?		

▶ **Dink**

The **dink** (tip) is executed with all the movements associated with the basic spike. The actual ball contact, however, is quite different. The speed of the arm is dramatically reduced, and the widespread fingers place the ball over the blockers' outstretched hands.

THE QUICK ATTACK

A **quick attack** in the middle is designed to create a one-on-one attack/block situation so that there is a substantive possibility to create an ineffective block or an attack that is unblocked. The approach is slightly angled, so that the hitter directly approaches the setter, starting the approach as the setter is contacting the ball. The

Checklist 4

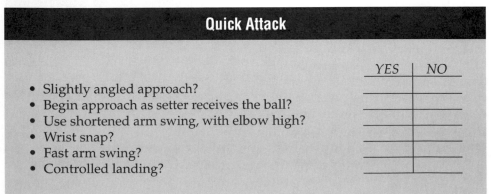

Quick Attack		
	YES	*NO*
• Slightly angled approach?		
• Begin approach as setter receives the ball?		
• Use shortened arm swing, with elbow high?		
• Wrist snap?		
• Fast arm swing?		
• Controlled landing?		

attacker uses a shortened arm swing, with the elbow held high, and extremely limited use of the non-hitting arm in the approach. Wrist snap is critical for success. The faster the arm swing, the more forceful will be the attack.

BACK ROW ATTACK

A **back row attack** is another offensive technique that has provided greater variety to the game of volleyball. It allows the offense to utilize a powerful hit that disturbs the first line of defense, the block.

There are two basic skills involved in the back-row attack: the set which literally facilitates the attack, and the attack itself. The set must be approximately 5 m high (15′) and peak just in front of the 3 m line. There is no basic difference in its execution, other than the setter's shoulders may be turned slightly into the court rather than being squared to the left sideline. The attacker has less room for error, since the ball is set approximately 3 m (9′) from the net. Therefore, the consistency of the set is vitally important to the success of the back row attack.

The approach and contact point are slightly different than the traditional front zone attack. The player must approach powerfully and will travel in a more forward direction. The jump must occur from behind the 3 m line, as the attacker is usually a member of the back row. The player will use the arms to forcefully assist in the jump, and will arch the back slightly more in order to contact the ball underneath and slightly closer to the body so as to provide enough lift on the ball to get it over the net with power and spin.

Checklist 5

Back Row Attack		
	YES	NO
• Point of takeoff behind the 3 m line?		
• Angle of approach more forward than traditional attack?		
• Double arm swing?		
• Contact ball just in front of body?		
• Back arch?		
• Contact ball at top of jump?		
• Full arm extension and wrist snap?		
• Slight travel forward upon balanced landing?		

THE BACK SLIDE ATTACK

The **back slide attack,** where the player takes off from one foot and is moving the same direction as the ball, opens up a range of possibilities for the player that defies single blocks and reduces the effectiveness of double blocks. The player, when using the slide attack, can beat the block by attacking the ball in a variety of positions within a window of opportunity established at approximately 1 m (3') in width along the net.

Fundamental to slide attacks are five major concepts. First, the attacker, at take-off, should move parallel to the set trajectory. Therefore, the player is running parallel to the net when the final plant step and the jump occur. The attacker must approach the net and then curve toward the sideline, creating a curve which is concave to the net. Second, the player must accelerate into the run and through the jump. This concept is similar to that which a long jumper uses to convert horizontal into somewhat vertical movement. Third, the player must accelerate the approach so that the ball is not only caught up to, but is passed along its and the player's trajectory. The player will contact the ball as it is passed. Fourth, the attacker must rotate the body as the jump occurs and as the body is approaching the ball. The turn is begun from the planting of the lead foot, through the knee and hip. This adds substantial torque and force through the arm and hand to ultimately deliver tremendous power to the ball. Fifth, the attacker has a window of opportunity that is almost 1 m (3') wide. Ideally, the attacker would like to reach and swing to the ball within the window for the greatest effect. Because the player travels faster than the ball, the attack point can occur anywhere within the window.

To perform the back slide, begin in the middle of the court, in a neutral position, facing the net. Visualize the pattern in an arc on the floor. If right handed, accelerate left, right, left, bringing the right knee up, then landing on both feet. When the right knee comes up, the left foot is planted three to five feet from the beginning of

Checklist 6

Back Slide Attack

	YES	NO
• Starting the middle of the court?		
• Neutral position, facing the net?		
• Visualize a pattern in an arc on the floor?		
• L-R-L-bring R knee up and land on both feet?		

the attack window. As the player goes up, the body is traveling faster than the ball. The player has the opportunity to hit the ball in a fairly large window.

Three other concepts are important for ultimate success of the slide attack. The speed of the approach, or the time that it takes to complete the approach, is one variable to consider. Spacing, or the distance of the final plant foot from the point of the attack, is a second consideration, and timing, or the hitter's point in the approach when the setter touches the ball, also must be considered. These time and space considerations provide cues which are taken from the setter. For a first-tempo set, where the ball peaks one to two feet above the top of the net, the attacker crosses the left foot past the right leg into the last approach step when the ball comes into the setter's hands. For a second-tempo set, where the ball peaks three to four feet above the top of the net, the attacker should cross the right foot past the left leg in the next to the last step in the approach.

BASIC TYPES OF SETS

Setters have the opportunity to orchestrate a variety of attacks that are generated from a variety of sets. Below are six basic types of sets which can be used in various situations presented in games. Play sets can be part of an **audible offense,** one that is verbalized as a set or play pattern to the team.

1 set   Known as a quick set or short set, it is generally located one foot above and in the middle area of the net. The ball is generally contacted before it has reached the peak of its trajectory.

2 set   Known also as a low set, it can be either front or back. It is generally two to four feet above and in the middle area of the net. The ball is generally contacted just before it reaches the apex of its trajectory.

3 set   Known as a medium height set, it is four to six feet above the net. It is generally positioned halfway from the setter and the sideline. The ball is generally contacted just after it reaches the apex of its trajectory.

4 set   Known as a shoot set, it runs nearly parallel to the top of the net. Its height is one to two feet above the net. The ball is contacted before it reaches the apex of its trajectory.

5 set   Known as a back set to the outside of the court, ball height is about ten feet above the net. The ball is contacted well after it reaches the apex of its trajectory.

6 set   Known as a high outside set, it is also a front set to the outside sideline. Ten feet above the net, the ball is contacted well after it reaches the apex of its trajectory.

The following are examples of play sets that can be utilized during games. Play sets are first numbered by the zone and then by the type of the set. Of course, the notion of play sets is predicated on the success of the team to pass to Zone 5, or the area where the setter is most apt to successfully perform quality setting.

16 = a high outside set to Zone 1, or to the left sideline
41 = a quick front set to Zone 4 for a middle attack
31 = a front set of medium height to Zone 3
75 = a high back set to the outside

The skills of spiking and serving are initiated by players' actions. The players are in control of their performances. Therefore, each hitter needs to be able to perform a variety of attack techniques in order to keep the defensive players challenged. These attacks include hitting down the line, crosscourt, over the block, or the seam (of a zone) or wiping the block.

Hitting the line, crosscourt, and over the block have already been discussed. **Wiping the block or tooling the block,** is a technique used to have the ball rebound out of the court off of the blockers' hands. By turning the thumb down and cutting the ball into the block, the ball's trajectory should go out of bounds and out of play.

MULTIPLE BLOCKING

Double blocking takes away a good portion of the court from the attacker if the block is set appropriately. The end or **outside blocker** generally sets the block. The player must decide where to position the block by watching the set and the hitter's approach and keying on the armswing. The outside blocker positions the inside hand on the ball to take away the down-the-line attack. The middle blocker, using a crossover step, closes the block. The outside blocker times the jump so that both blockers go up simultaneously.

The crossover step is the quickest technique by which to cover the distance along the net, particularly when the opponents utilize the quick attack. In the ready position, the blocker waits to see the direction of the set. Moving to the left sideline from the middle is begun by stepping with the right foot across and in front of the left pivot foot. This turns the shoulders away from the net. The right foot plants, closely followed by the left. By firmly planting the left foot when jumping, lateral movement is converted into vertical and drift is kept to a minimum. Movement to the right sideline reverses the procedure.

FIGURE 9-6 Outside blockers focus on the ball; middle blockers take away the angle. Courtesy of D. Kluka

Checklist 7

Blocking		
	YES	*NO*
• Outside blocker sets the block?		
• Outside blocker times the jump so that both blockers go up simultaneously?		
• Firmly plant the first foot when jumping?		

FIGURE 9-7 Double block sequence. Courtesy of D. Kluka.

SUMMARY

- The most sophisticated and complex serve is the jump serve. The server can produce extraordinary velocities and a lower trajectory of delivery.
- Two factors contribute to the success of serving any ball. First, the palm should face toward the target. Second, by looking down the arm at contact, the ball should appear to fly in a trajectory in line with the arm.
- The jump set can be used to create the fastest play in the game of volleyball. When it is combined with a quick middle attack, it serves to force the middle blocker to commit to the middle attack.

- As a setter, attacking the ball over the net on the second contact after deceiving the opponents with a preliminary setting motion can be effective. The setter attack can be successfully used when a back court defensive player is deep in the court.
- The dink or tip is executed with all the movements associated with the basic spike. The speed of the arm is dramatically reduced, and the widespread fingers place the ball over the blockers' outstretched hands.
- A quick attack in the middle is designed to create a one-on-one attack/block situation so that there is a substantive possibility to create an ineffective block or an attack that is unblocked. The approach is slightly angled so that the hitter directly approaches the setter, starting the approach as the setter is contacting the ball.
- A back row attack allows the offense to utilize a powerful hit that disturbs the first line of defense, the block.
- The back slide attack, where the player takes off from one foot and is moving the same direction as the ball, opens up a range of possibilities for the player that defies single blocks and reduces the effectiveness of double blocks. The player, when using the slide attack, can beat the block by attacking the ball in a variety of positions within a window of opportunity established at approximately 1 m in width along the net.
- Double blocking takes away a good portion of the court from the attacker if the block is set appropriately. The outside blocker positions the inside hand on the ball to take away the down-the-line attack.

▶ **jump serve   p. 146**
an advanced skill that provides variety for the offense and produces angular velocities in excess of 23 m/s or 52 mph

▶ **jump set   p. 149**
reduces the time it takes for the ball to get from the setter to the attacker

▶ **setter attack   p. 150**
setter tipping the ball over the net on the second contact

▶ **dink (tip)   p. 152**
the attacker's arm speed is dramatically reduced to place the ball over the blocker's outstretched hands

▶ **quick attack   p. 152**
an attack from the middle which is designed to create a one-on-one attack/block situation

▶ **back row attack   p. 153**
this type of attack allows the offense to utilize a powerful hit that disturbs the first line of defense

▶ **back slide attack   p. 154**
the player takes off from one foot and is moving the same direction as the ball

▶ **audible offense   p. 155**
an offense that is verbalized as a set or play pattern to the team

▶ **outside blocker   p. 156**
a player in the LF or RF position and who usually sets the block

▶ **wiping or tooling the block   p. 156**
a technique used to have the ball rebound out of the court off of the blocker's hands

Assessment 9-1

Name _____ Section _____ Date _____

Jump Serve for Accuracy and Speed.

Equipment: Server; cart of balls; ball shaggers.

Description: Stand anywhere along the endline to serve. Jump serve as many balls as possible within the time frame. Count the number of serves you get over the net and in the court.

Goal: See how many serves will go over the net and land in-bounds within two minutes.

Your performance: _____.

Assessment 9-2

Name   Section   Date

Pass-Set-Quick Hit

Equipment: Ten balls; court; passer; setter; attacker.

Description: Toss a ball over the net to a passer who overhead passes the ball to the setter, who jump sets the quick attack. To vary this, begin from serve reception positions.

Goal: The ball that is attacked lands within fifteen feet of the net, seven out of ten attempts.

Your group's performance: _____.

Assessment 9-3

Name   Section   Date

Equipment: Three boxes; four players; cart of balls.

Description: Three blockers are up at the net. Three attackers are positioned on boxes opposite the blockers. Left-side attacker spikes crosscourt with the middle blocker working on one-on-one; the middle hitter spikes the power angle with the middle blocker blocking one-on-one. Upon landing, the middle blocker joins the right side blocker as the left side hitter tries to hit between the block. The left blocker comes off the net to pick up the sharp angle or dink. Repeat the same steps to the opposite side.

Goal: Complete a total of six attacks and blocks per set, with five sets per group.

Your performance: _____.

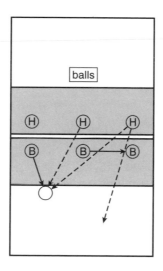

ADVANCED
PLAYING SYSTEMS:
OFFENSIVE AND DEFENSIVE

OBJECTIVES

After reading this chapter, you should be able to do the following:

- Understand team composition and what goes into selecting a team based upon position and function.
- Understand the International 4–2, 6–2, and 5–1 offensive systems.
- Select an offensive system that is conducive to the abilities of those on the team.
- Understand attacker coverage, free ball situations, and serve reception based on multiple offensive systems.

KEY TERMS

While reading this chapter, you will become familiar with the following terms:

- ▶ International 4–2 offensive system
- ▶ 6–2 offensive system
- ▶ 5–1 offensive system
- ▶ substitute

There are a variety of offensive systems that display a higher level of sophistication for the game of volleyball. Among the most commonly used are the International 4–2, the 6–2, and the 5–1.

INTERNATIONAL OFFENSIVE SYSTEM

The **4–2 international offensive system,** like the traditional 4–2, has four designated attackers and two setters. The front court setter, however, is positioned on the right front side of the court rather than in the center of the court. The two front court attackers are positioned in the middle and left front zones of the court.

The concept of the middle attack is utilized in this system. The attack can be quite effective, creating a one-on-one situation between offense and defense (one attacker/one blocker). Teams using the traditional 4–2 system have their setters as middle blockers. This usually creates a height mismatch between hitter and blocker, the hitter having the advantage.

The ultimate position of the front court setter is approximately eight feet from the right sideline close to the net. The two front court attackers will be hitting from the left and center zones of the court. This places more responsibility on the opposing middle blocker. Blocking priorities are to prevent the middle attack first, then move to block the outside left attack.

SERVE RECEPTION

This system closely resembles the W-formation used in the traditional 4–2 system discussed in Chapter 8. Setters begin in the RF and LB positions. This permits the front zone setter to begin in a rotation where no switching needs to occur.

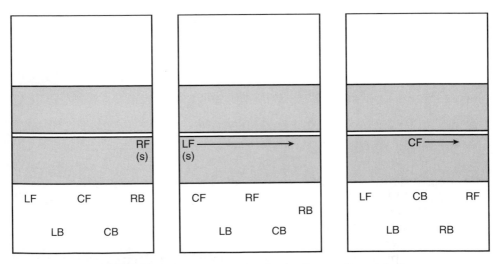

FIGURE 10-1 Serve reception in the International 4–2.

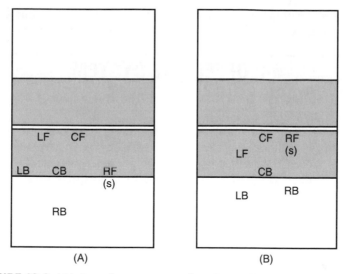

(A)   (B)

FIGURE 10-2 (A) Attack coverage when LF is the attacker, using the International 4–2. (B) Attack coverage when CF is the attacker.

ATTACKER COVERAGE

Attacker coverage for the International 4–2 is again similar to the traditional 4–2. Three players create a semicircle around the attacker. The two other players split the space in between. The CB forms the centerpiece of the semicircle. The LB and CF form the remainder of the semicircle if the attack is generated from the left; the RB and RF serve to fill in the spaces. When the attack is from the middle, the LF, RF, and CB create the semicircle, while the LB and RB fill in the spaces.

FREE BALL

The free ball position is virtually the same as the traditional 4–2 system. Two attackers are switched to the CF and LF positions. The setter is in the RF position. Therefore, the RB moves forward, while the CB moves back and to the right to cover deep.

One of the most versatile offensive systems in the game of volleyball involves the concept of bringing the setter from the back court, thereby creating

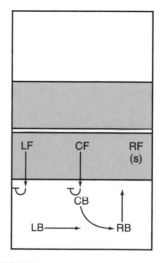

FIGURE 10-3 Basic defense to free ball position in the International 4–2.

opportunities for a full range of attack possibilities at the LF, CF, and RF positions. Two of the most successful systems have been the 6–2 and 5–1 offenses.

6-2 OFFENSIVE SYSTEM
(BACK COURT SETTER SYSTEM)

Six players possessing the ability to play a spiking role, two of whom can also function as setters, are necessary to execute the **6–2 offensive system.** The system always utilizes the primary setter from the back court; this permits greater variation in attack options. This also enhances outside and quick middle attacks and makes blocking more challenging for the opponents.

SERVE RECEPTION

An objective of the 6–2 system is to get the setter into the front court before the served ball has crossed the net. The following "W" and "U" service reception patterns indicate the basic positions for players using a 6–2 offensive system.

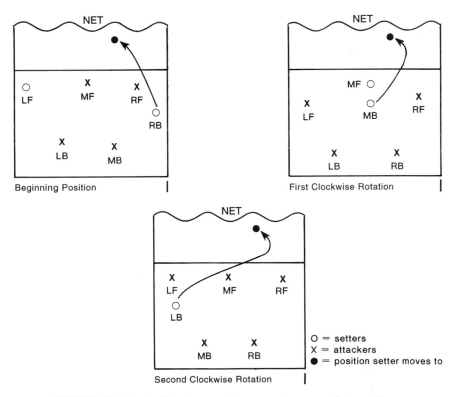

FIGURE 10-4 6–2 offensive system service reception pattern.

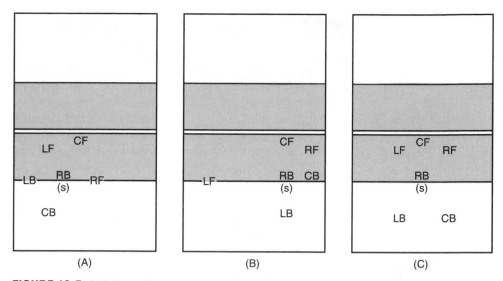

FIGURE 10-5 (A) Attacker coverage, when the LF is attacking in the 6–2 offense system. (B) Attacker coverage, when the RF is attacking in the 6–2 offense system. (C) Attacker coverage, when the CF is attacking in the 6–2 offense system.

In the second rotation, the left back has the greatest distance to travel. It is important for the setter to allow the middle front and middle back to clearly see the oncoming serve prior to moving into position. The pass must be the first priority of the team, not the setter's initial movement.

ATTACKER COVERAGE

The 3–2 player concept used in previous attacker coverage can again be considered with the 6–2. The players responsible for that coverage, however, are quite different. In the 6–2 system, the setter is the centerpiece of the three-player semicircle. The CF is always closest to the net if the attack is generated from the left or right side. Once the ball is put into play, despite the rotations, the setter remains in the RB position. This makes practical sense, as the distance that must be traveled by the setter to the setting position is least. The RB area is also one that is least vulnerable to attack, as it is not generally part of the power attack zone.

FREE BALL

All three attackers back up off the net when a free ball is called. The setter moves quickly to the net from the position of RB. The CB moves up and to the right to balance the court. The LB moves to the right to also balance the court.

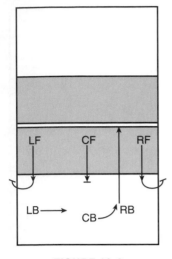

FIGURE 10-6

5–1 MULTIPLE OFFENSIVE SYSTEM

The 5–1 offensive system is a combination of the 4–2 and 6–2 offensive systems. Five players are designated as attackers; one player functions as the setter. Consistency of setting is one advantage to this system. It is used most frequently at the elite international level.

As the setter moves from the back court, a 6–2 system pattern is used. When the setter is in the front court, the 4–2 system is employed.

The most versatile player is placed opposite the setter. Once the ball is served, the best blocker assumes the middle position when in the front court. The following 5- and 4-player service reception patterns indicate the basic positions for teams using a 5–1 offensive system. (See Figures 10-7 and 10-8.)

ATTACKER COVERAGE

Attacker coverage resembles the 6–2 offensive system coverage when the setter comes from the back zone. When the setter is in the front zone, the coverage is the same as that used in the International 4–2 system. The concept of 3–2 coverage is where three players position themselves in a semicircle and the other two balance the court in between.

FREE BALL

The 5–1 system and 6–2 system resemble one another when the setter comes from the back zone and the same as the International 4–2 when the setter is in the front zone.

SPECIALIZATION

Finally, selection of appropriate players for positions and functions that provide the team with its greatest strengths should be a top priority once skills are learned. The general thought associated with specialization of team responsibilities is that the more highly specialized a player is, the greater the chance of proficiency in the performance of the skills required. The physical and mental as well as the technical components need to be identified. In the early chapters of this

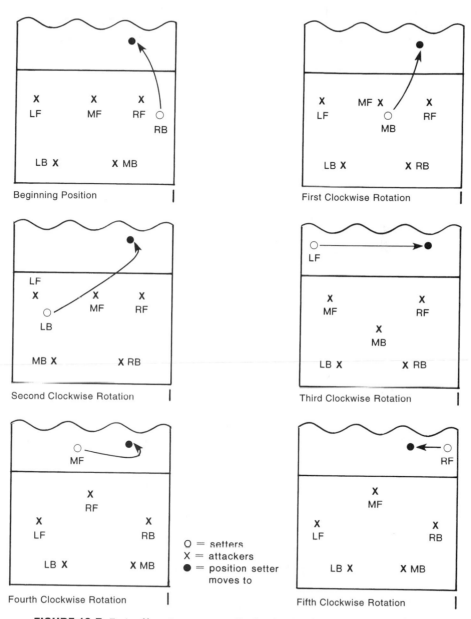

FIGURE 10-7 5–1 offensive system 5-player service reception pattern.

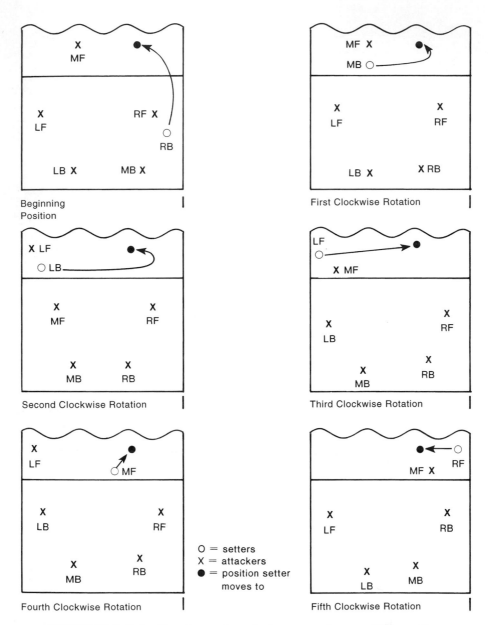

FIGURE 10-8 5–1 offensive system 4-player service reception pattern.

text, the technical components of each of the skills necessary for volleyball were identified.

TEAM COMPOSITION

The rules of the game place certain limits upon players. For example, an individual may play three rotations in the front court (left front, middle front, right front) and three rotations in the back court (left back, middle back, right back). While in the front court, the player may attack and block; while in the back court, the player may not block, but may attack the ball as long as takeoff is from behind the 3 m line or part of the ball is below the height of the net.

▶ Specialization by Position

Within rule limits, it seems that a player could specialize in front court position and back court position—left, right, center. This specialization is accomplished by *position*. By playing only one position in the front court (offense) and one in the back court (defense), numerous variables are reduced to a few, thereby giving each player a better chance at proficiency. In order to do this, players must switch positions during the game. Switching can be accomplished at several different times during the game: (1) immediately after the serve, (2) during and after serve reception, and (3) during and after the attack.

▶ Specialization by Function

Another way of specializing is by *function*: (1) setting and (2) attacking. Each team member becomes either a setter or an attacker. Because defense must be played by position, each member can then learn two defensive positions, one in the front court, one in the back court.

A *setter* orchestrates the team's attack. The following characteristics are beneficial to a setter:

- considered a play maker for the team,
- able to decide which attacker to set,
- cool under pressure but can inspire other team members,
- able to communicate with the other players, and the coach,
- the most versatile and skilled individual on the team, and
- able to move the feet quickly and hit the ball with either hand; demonstrates quick eye movements and extended peripheral vision.

The *center* or *middle* players are referred to as middle blockers/middle hitters (or quick attackers) (Figure 10-10—M_1 and M_2). When serving this function, a middle player should:

- participate in almost every block; therefore, a player must have good jumping ability and should be the best blocker on the team,
- never give up and move quickly and assertively during each play,

- have excellent peripheral vision and court awareness, because there is a vulnerability to all areas of the court,
- initiate quick attacks and off-speed shots in order to create opportunities to exploit the defensive team's weaknesses, and
- use good technical skills and speed rather than relying upon force alone.

The *power attacker* (Figure 10-10—P_1 and P_2) functions as the strong attack from the left side of the court if the player is right-handed. The power attacker should:

- be one of the best jumpers on the team,
- be able to hit the ball with tremendous force so points can be scored from the attack,
- exhibit self-confidence on the court,
- be able to wipe (tool) the block so the ball goes out-of-bounds off of the block, and
- set the block accurately when the team uses a double block.

An *option player* (Figure 10-10—O_1 and O_2) is one who attacks from the right front position. To be successful, the option player should:

- be left-handed; this creates the option of having two primary attackers, one on each side of the court,
- be able to move and adjust from offense to defense quickly, and
- serve as a good substitute, depending upon which offensive system the team is using, the option player may be substituted into the front court to replace a short setter.

FIGURE 10-9 A power attacker provides excitement to the offense. Courtesy of B. Blanford.

Generally, the *power attacker* plays the left front and left back positions. The *middle-blocker* usually plays the middle front and middle back positions. *Setters* or *option players* play right front and right back positions. By using this as a basis for team composition, the team has the opportunity to utilize specific talents of each team member and play to their strengths.

▶ The Role of the Effective Substitute

Being a **substitute** is a reality and a necessity when playing on a volleyball team. How a substitute is handled not only affects the player but may determine the success or failure of the team. Many games are won or lost because of the

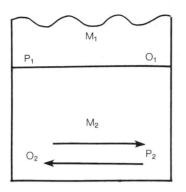

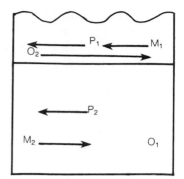

Initial Rotation

Second Clockwise Rotation

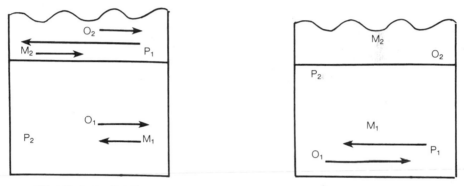

Third Clockwise Rotation

Fourth Clockwise Rotation

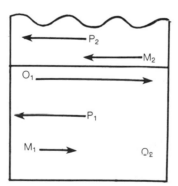

Fifth Clockwise Rotation

FIGURE 10-10 Team composition: specialization. Upon service of the ball, players switch positions so that they can specialize in playing one position. As a back row player, for example, player O, in the second, third, and fourth clockwise rotations, switches to the right back (RB) position until the end of each play.

performance of a substitute. If a substitute is to be effective, he or she must understand the significance of the role and accept the responsibility of contributing to the team's success in a supportive capacity. Common roles that a substitute plays include server, back court specialist, right side blocker, and middle back defender.

A substitute must be ready to enter the game at any moment. This requires both physical and mental readiness. The substitute enters the game at a point when some type of change is needed, and the enthusiasm conveyed to the rest of the team is vital.

The substitute must always work diligently to become a starter. Positive contributions during practice and games can substantially affect the player's contribution to the team's success.

Substitutes must study the game from the sideline. Players need to have accurate perceptions of when and where their strengths as substitutes are likely to be utilized. Being able to locate weak passers, blockers, and attackers can be quite a contribution to the team's success. Looking for defensive weaknesses as well as offensive tendencies can greatly help the team. Discovering telegraphing movements made by the opposing team's setter and deciding how best to take advantage of the opponent's weaknesses can be determined from the sideline.

By using mental imagery techniques prior to entry into a game, moments where substitution may occur can be "seen." Including internal variables (feelings of anxiety, listening to heartbeat and breathing), as well as external cues (crowd noise, referees' actions, coaches' responses) can assist in simulating specific court situations. An appropriate movement response from each situation can be rehearsed by the substitute before entering the court.

There is no shame in being a substitute. The team is only as strong as its least effective substitute. Contributions are of vital importance to the team. Being positive, working diligently, and performing appropriately in all situations will become an integral part of the team's success.

SUMMARY

- The International 4–2 system has four designated attackers and two setters. The front court setter is positioned on the right front side of the court. The two front court attackers are positioned in the middle and left front zones of the court.
- The 6–2 offensive system allows six players the ability to spike, two of them also function as setters. The primary setter comes from the back court, thereby permitting greater variation in attack options.
- Player specialization can occur by position and by function.
- Being a substitute is a reality and a necessity when playing on a volleyball team. The substitute must be ready to enter the game at any moment and must work diligently to become a starter.

▶ **International 4–2 offensive system**   p. 166
four designated attackers and two setters

▶ **6–2 offensive system**   p. 168
all players act as attackers when in the front zone; the primary setter always comes from the back court

▶ **5–1 offensive system**   p. 170
5 designated attackers and 1 setter; combination of front and back row setter system

▶ **substitute**   p. 174
player who enters the game after it has begun to replace someone who is in the lineup

Assessment 10-1

Name   Section   Date

TEAM SCORING

1. Fast Score

   A point is scored on every play. There are no sideouts. Play to twenty-five and then rotate.

2. Handicap

   One team has more points than the other at the onset. (Example: Score is already five to zero.) Game to ten.

3. Wash

   A team must score at least two small points in a row to score one large point. To win a small game, a team must score so many large points. To win a large game, a team must win so many small games. Option: a team must win by two large points to win a small game and by two small games to win the large game.

4. Baseball

   A game is comprised of six innings. A team can score only when at bat (serving). Each server gets three outs. If the receiving team sides out, it is counted as one out. It the serving team scores a point, the team gets a free ball. The team at bat scores a point for each free ball killed. The team keeps getting free balls until it is stopped by either the other team or by error. If points are scored, the server does not lose that serve opportunity. When the receiving team gets three side outs, it rotates and serves (or comes to bat).

Assessment 10-2

Name   Section   Date

DO IT ALL TOGETHER

Equipment: Court; team plus 3.

Description: The ball is served by Player A. The receiving team (Players B, C, D, E, F and G) passes and runs an offensive play against three blockers (Players H, I, J). If the ball is successfully attacked, the tosser tosses a ball to the setter on the tosser's side. The tosser's team counterattacks with an offensive play. The receiving team, now in defensive position, defends against the attack and attempts to counterattack. The drill continues as long as the receiving team does not make an error. At the tosser's discretion, a ball may be tossed to either one of the diggers (K and L) on the tosser's team to have them pass a free ball to the receiving team, who must adjust accordingly.

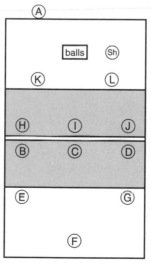

Sh = Shagger

Appendix A

Volleyball Officiating

Volleyball officiating is a common sense application of the rules to a competitive event. It is usually performed in an environment that demands complete accuracy with speed and finesse.

Officiating is performed by an officiating team. The team is composed of a first referee, a second referee, a scorekeeper, and two or four line judges. The rules list each official's responsibilities. Some of these necessarily are specific to one official. Some are shared. An effective officiating team is one in which each official does the job well and is alert to being able to assist and support the other officials, if help is requested. A pre-match conference enables the officials to review how they will work together.

The first referee, the primary official, is positioned on an elevated stand across the court from the team benches and the scorekeeping table. This official is in charge of the officiating team. Judgment decisions by this official are final. The first referee has the authority to settle all questions, including those not specifically covered in the rules. The official may overrule the decision of another official, if it is felt that the official made an error. Primary responsibilities include: (1) controlling the start of play, (2) deciding on the legality of ball handling, (3) ruling on any infraction that occurs during play, (4) deciding when to assess a penalty, and (5) signaling to participants and to spectators what has just taken place.

The second referee is positioned on the floor across from the first referee. The second referee is responsible for timely substitutions, net and centerline violations, and support for the first referee.

The scorekeeper maintains the official record of the score and informs the second referee of substitutions, serving order, and time outs. This official sits at the official scorekeeping table.

Line judges call balls in or out that are close to their assigned sidelines or endlines, according to the instructions they receive during the prematch officiating conference. They also determine if a ball crosses the net, is not completely inside the net antenna, or touches a nonplayable object, such as a basketball backboard. They signal when they see a ball touched by a player. They may assist on decisions involving whether a ball touched the floor. Each of these topics is reviewed during the pre-match conference.

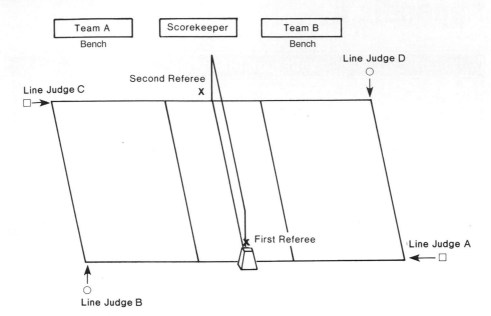

The officiating team shown above has four line judges. If only two line judges are used, they are positioned as in A and C in the diagram and are responsible for the endline closer to them as well as for the designated sideline.

CHARACTERISTICS OF THE IDEAL VOLLEYBALL OFFICIAL

One of the proven ways of generating participation in a volleyball officials' clinic is to have the group name and prioritize the characteristics that the ideal official possesses. The reaction is almost always the same, but the order of priority may vary slightly. These characteristics include desire, knowledge, integrity, courage, consistency, concentration, reaction, anticipation, leadership, mechanics, appearance, and personality.

DESIRE

The ideal official wants to do the best job possible. The individual is willing to spend time and resources to learn how to become an effective official and to practice and perfect these skills as frequently as possible.

KNOWLEDGE

The ideal official knows the rules of the game, the current interpretation of the rules, and the appropriate method of their implementation. Rules are updated frequently. It is important for every official to have a copy of the current rule book for the specific type of competition.

INTEGRITY

The ideal official is honest, objective, and impartial. There is no attempt to impress someone at the risk of jeopardizing the accuracy of the decisions rendered. There is no attempt to make up for a previously missed call. There is a willingness to reverse a ruling, to make the correct call, even if it is a late call.

Signaling the service by the first referee. Courtesy of the University of Central Oklahoma Photographic Service.

COURAGE

The ideal official has the courage to do the right thing even though it may not be popular with competitors or spectators. The individual is willing to accept criticism and translate it into ways of improving officiating proficiency.

CONSISTENCY

The ideal official maintains the same high standards of quality through the match. If rules (e.g., ball handling judgment) are implemented strictly or permissively at the beginning of the match, the official will continue to administer the competition with the same strict or permissive judgmental criteria until the match has been completed.

CONCENTRATION/REACTION/ANTICIPATION

The ideal official is alert to what has just happened and what is happening right now and has the ability to accurately anticipate what may happen. Reaction to what has happened or is happening must be correct and prompt. Anticipation is an attribute that must be utilized with control. It enables the good official to react appropriately and promptly. Many good officials, however, have failed at some time to control anticipation and whistled prematurely. For example, the ball, which no one could probably get to, is whistled as "down" before it actually hits the floor, and the whistle is immediately followed by an outstanding defensive play by some player who could not, but did, manage to retrieve it. Replay is the appropriate call. Anticipating accurately gives the official an edge on reacting, but it must be used prudently and only as a possibility of what may happen.

Officiating techniques include keeping the whistle in the mouth during play. Courtesy of D. Kluka.

LEADERSHIP

The ideal official is willing to make a decision. Calls are made decisively in a manner that evokes the confidence of players, coaches, and other officials. Although decisive, each call conveys certainty and is unemotional. There is no grandstanding. The official is able to utilize the talents of the other officials effectively by involving them in the competition, respecting/obtaining their judgment on those calls that fall into their respective areas of responsibility according to the rules and prescribed officiating techniques.

MECHANICS/TECHNIQUES

The ideal official follows the prescribed mechanics and techniques documented in the rule book. This includes such items as utilizing only standard hand signals, blowing the whistle with authority and in a timely fashion, moving to the proper position, supervising bench conduct, interacting tactfully and courteously with participants, communicating effectively with other officials, and observing specified protocol.

CONDITION/APPEARANCE

The ideal official must have 20/20 eyesight, either uncorrected or corrected, and physical condition must provide the necessary stamina to conduct the match

Sideout or change of service.

Ball landing within the court boundaries and ball under net.

Ball out-of-bounds.

Touches on ball landing out-of-bounds.

Ball contacted more than three times.

Player crossing the center line.

Frequently used officiating signals. Courtesy of NAGWS.

Illegal hit.

Double hit.

Substitution.

Team sanctions: team delay (e.g., warning).

Time out.

Begin service.

Net foul.

Replay.

Screening.

Reaching across the net.

Individual sanctions (e.g., warning).

Change of courts.

Point.

End of game or match.

effectively. Some collegiate matches have lasted three hours. Each official is attired in the uniform prescribed in the rule book. Presenting a professional image that instills confidence by neatness and cleanliness is fundamental. First impressions by players, coaches, and spectators are lasting ones.

PERSONALITY

The ideal official brings each of the previous characteristics together in a unique way that reflects credit on the sport and the official. Desirable personality traits include a genuine concern for each participant, a cooperative attitude, a sense of humor, the ability to control emotions, and finesse in handling differences of opinion.

BEGINNING AS AN OFFICIAL

Two major objectives in the process of learning to become an official are (1) to develop a basic understanding of the game and (2) to gain practical experience. Each game officiated contributes to the official's development. This is an ongoing process which ends only when the official ceases to grow and improve.

Developing a basic understanding includes getting a current rule book and learning the rules. It is important to learn what each rule literally means. It is also important to understand its purposes: to sustain play and to increase spectator interest by balancing the relative advantages of offensive and defensive action. Understanding the reason for the rule enables the official to administer it based upon instantaneous logical reaction.

Understanding the intricacy of volleyball rules can be facilitated by working with an experienced official or group of officials who can listen, answer questions, discuss game situations, critique performance, offer suggestions, and generally provide encouragement and support. The beginning official should contact the nearest officials' organization and become active in its developmental programs. The state high school association, local PAVO board, or USAV region can identify these human resources.

An additional way to learn about volleyball is to be active as a player. Although not absolutely essential to success, a prospective official with a playing background can appreciate what players and coaches expect from the person with the whistle. Officials with a playing background may find it easier to follow game action and strategies. The level of play in which this experience is gained is not as important as the fact that it is a competitive environment that includes game officials.

To further understand the sport, attendance at one or more early season practices of a college team is beneficial. The purpose of the visit is to witness the intense work expended by the coaches and players in conditioning and in perfecting the technical skills. A person who has this experience may better appreciate the importance of the referee's responsibilities.

This referee follows the ball with his eyes during play. Courtesy of D. Kluka.

Practical experience is a necessity in the making of a good volleyball official. Local parks and recreation departments often conduct adult recreational programs in the evening. Even if there is a regular official, it is possible that there is need for a volunteer to act as the "down" official (second referee). College intramural programs also frequently need officials. The intramural director is the individual to contact for assistance. During the first two weeks of the high school season (before interscholastic competition begins), there are opportunities to volunteer to referee a high school intrasquad scrimmage. Sanctioned USAV tournaments frequently utilize members from teams not playing in a match to officiate the games between two participating clubs. A volunteer is welcome. The regional commissioner can provide information about times and sites of tournaments.

COMMON SENSE IDEAS ABOUT OFFICIATING

Volleyball is played at many levels, from the "backyard variety" to international competition. The official has a major impact upon whether the program achieves its objectives. The objective may be primarily social/recreational, the development of playing techniques, or strictly competitive. Because there is an official assigned, the organizers of the event have certain expectations. It is important for the official to understand what these expectations are. In a socially competitive environment, an official may be able to be more lenient in interpreting the rules. For example, rules regarding uniform specifications may be relaxed. In contrast, the same official may contribute more to a high school freshman team's learning and development through very strict rule interpretation, which will be a more effective learning experience. Rules regarding the wearing of jewelry may need to be rigidly enforced for safety reasons. Experienced officials will cooperate closely with coaches so their officiating is accepted as an additional training resource.

In some situations the standard hand signals may need amplification by verbalization. An official should feel comfortable in explaining the call when such explanation is appropriate.

The official's role in the game is to have the competition progress in an orderly fashion through consistent administration of the rules. Each rule violation is called, but the effective official helps the competition progress by preventing the rule from being violated. This positive trait is called preventative officiating.

Preventative officiating includes such courtesies as observing the players' equipment and attire and pointing out to the coach any item that does not comply with the rules. Such action prevents a penalty from being imposed after the competition has begun. It includes telling the coach how many time outs have been taken and when a player enters the game for the final permitted time. It may include asking the receiving team if its players can see the server, thereby reducing the possibility of a screen by the serving team. Preventative officiating might include the down official being in close proximity to the team's huddle and reminding its players that it is time to move back on the court so they are not penalized for a delay of game. This might be especially important if that team was almost tardy in returning during a prior time out. Preventative officiating (or possibly an officiating technique) might also involve complimenting support officials about how they are making their own contribution to preventative officiating. Everyone appreciates a well-deserved compliment, and the compliment positively reinforces the prematch discussion that outlines each support official's duties. For instance, the high school timer has sounded the horn promptly fifteen seconds before the end of each timeout period, and that assistance is recognized. The deserved thank you during the match will encourage continued effective assistance and, in turn, will help the official.

Preventative officiating, however, does not include the act of stopping a player from committing a foul while the game is in progress. For example, the incorrect player rotates to serve. The team is responsible for knowing the correct server. The officials do not warn the team that it is going to serve out of order. If the wrong player serves, the team loses the ball.

Preventative officiating minimizes the chance of violations occurring. It does not include telling the team that it is about to be penalized. The official who is using common sense in dealing impartially with both teams will have fewer problems.

MANAGING A COMPETITIVE ENVIRONMENT

Sporting events repeatedly contain incidents in which officials have been involved in an argument or disagreement with a player or coach. Emotional outbursts involving items thrown, players fighting, or officials subjected to demeaning and insulting language or actions can and do occur. Many spectators may be fascinated and/or amused by the antics of those involved. The baseball manager who kicks dirt all over the errant umpire's shoes and trousers, the basketball coach who gets so upset that he misses his chair when trying to sit down and sits unceremoniously on the floor, the football coach who tears apart the down marking device, or the volleyball coach who slams the clipboard to the floor and shoots verbal and/or visual daggers across the court at the official are examples of those antics. These actions seem to condone or encourage confrontation. As the sport of volleyball continues to develop, as attendance increases and the pressure to win becomes more intense, the official's management of the competitive environment becomes more important than ever.

There is no specific remedy for each situation that develops throughout the season. Each occurrence will have its own cast of characters with their moods and temperaments and specific events that immediately precede the disagreement. The creation of a positive competitive environment is of primary importance to the good official.

High school rules are very specific about the conduct of the participants, so their implementation is rather straightforward. In college and open (USAV) play, the rules prohibit any coaching activity that has a disruptive influence on the match. A deliberate delay of the game or a show of disgust in an overt manner are examples. The collegiate or open play official is left to judge what is considered to be disruptive.

In collegiate or open play competition, a coach or player should be allowed to express a normal positive or negative reaction to what has just happened. A positive competitive environment permits an occasional and spontaneous negative emotional reaction. The important words here are *occasional* and *spontaneous*. Repetitious or sustained outbursts should not be tolerated and should be penalized promptly. There may be an occasion in which a coach or player reacts so strongly that maintaining a positive competitive environment calls for an immediate penalty.

If there is controversy, the experienced official will move in immediately and diplomatically defuse the situation. This job is usually handled by the down official. A good first step in "Operation Defuse" is to listen. Step two is to clarify the call. (The difference of opinion may be prompted by a misunderstanding of the ruling.) At this critical point, the official should attempt to establish a balance between allowing a legitimate human reaction versus a common practice of penalizing immediately as a matter of normal officiating routine. Step three is to resume play as quickly as possible even if the last words spoken are "I'll be glad to discuss it further after the game."

It is important to analyze the reason the coach may be expressing a negative reaction to the official's decision. Is it really the decision that is being disputed, or is it the team's play? The coach may be reacting spontaneously and letting off steam; the coach may want to influence the call or try to motivate the team or break up the opponent's momentum. Motivating one's own team is positive. Upsetting the opponent's momentum through delay is negative. The other possible reasons cited may be either positive or negative. If the official feels the objective has a negative basis, a verbal warning may be used. If that fails, the yellow card, which serves as a warning, is an effective way to let the coach know that the demonstration has come to an end.

When controversy occurs, the official's responsibilities are to make the correct call; to facilitate understanding, if not complete acceptance; to cause the game to proceed in an orderly fashion without undue delay; and to maintain a professional image. Coaches and players may be allowed to react emotionally on occasion, but officials cannot. That is part of being an official in a competitive environment.

Appendix B

BOOKS/HANDBOOKS

Asher, K. S. (Ed.). (1995). *The Basic Elements of the Game: Best of Coaching Volleyball Series—Book One.* Indianapolis, IN: Masters Press.

Asher, K. S. (Ed.). (1996). *The Advanced Elements of the Game: Best of Coaching Volleyball Series—Book Two.* Indianapolis, IN: Masters Press.

Asher, K. S. (Ed.). (1996). *The Related Elements of the Game: Best of Coaching Volleyball Series—Book Three.* Indianapolis, IN: Masters Press.

Bertucci, R., & Hippolyte, R. (Eds.). (1984). *Championship Volleyball Drills (Vol. I).* Champaign, IL: Leisure Press.

Bertucci, R., & Kogut, T. (Eds.). (1985). *Championship Volleyball Drills (Vol. II).* Champaign, IL: Leisure Press.

Bertucci, R., & Peterson, J. (1992). *Volleyball Drill Book: Game Action Drills.* Indianapolis, IN: Masters Press.

Bertucci, R., & Peterson, J. (1992). *Volleyball Drill Book: Individual Skills.* Indianapolis, IN: Masters Press.

Davis, K. L. (1992). *Advanced Volleyball Everyone.* Winston-Salem, NC: Hunter Textbooks, Inc.

Federation Internationale de Volleyball. (1996). *One Hundred Years of Global Link: Volleyball Centennial, 1895–1995.* Milan, Italy: Staroffset, Cernusco S/N.

Gipson, M., Liskevych, N., & Liskevych, T. (1988). *Volleyball is a Hit: Pass, Serve, Dig, Set, Block.* Indianapolis, IN: Masters Press.

Homberg, S., & Papageorgiou, A. (1995). *Handbook for Beach Volleyball.* Aachen, Germany: Meyer & Meyer Verlag.

Keller, L., & Kluka, D. A. (1989). *Competitive Volleyball Drills for the Individual and Team.* Logan, UT: Kelcon.

Kluka, D., & Love, P. (1989). *Visual Skill Enhancement for Sport Exercise Cards.* Ruston, LA: *EyeSport,* Inc.

Kontor, K. (Ed.). (1996). *Complete Guide to Volleyball Conditioning.* Lincoln, NE: Conditioning Press.

McBride, J. (1991). Conditioning for Volleyball, 1(1). Lincoln, NE: National Strength and Conditioning Association.

McGown, C. (Ed.). (1994). *Science of Coaching Volleyball.* Champaign, IL: Human Kinetics Publishers.

National Association for Girls and Women in Sport Official Volleyball Rules. (Current). Reston, VA: AAHPERD Publications.

National High School Federation Official Volleyball Rules. (Current). Indianapolis, IN: NHSF Press.

Neville, W. J. (1990). *Coaching Volleyball Successfully.* Champaign, IL: Human Kinetics Publishers.

Smith, S. (1993). Play, play, play . . . *Volleyball, (7),* 44–46.

Smith, S., & Feineman, N. (1988). *Kings of the Beach: The Story of Beach Volleyball.* Los Angeles, CA: Seattle.

Viera, B. L., & Ferguson, B. J. (1989). *Volleyball: Steps to Success.* Champaign, IL: Human Kinetics Publishers.

JOURNALS/MAGAZINES/NEWSLETTERS

Coaching Volleyball Journal—Technical journal published by the American Volleyball Coaches Association

International Journal of Volleyball Research—Refereed research journal published by USA Volleyball

The Coach—Technical magazine published by the Federation Internationale de Volleyball

Volleyball USA—Newsletter published by USA Volleyball about USA Volleyball programs

VOLLEYBALL NETWORKS

Websites:
www.usavolleyball.org—Created in 1994, it is the homepage of USA Volleyball. National team information, youth and junior program information, regional office and member organization links, coaching and officiating information, FAQs, beach and disabled volleyball opportunities.

www.fivb.ch—The home page for the Federation Internationale de Volleyball (FIVB). It features both indoor and beach games. Information is also available on the World Championships, World League, Grand Prix, and World Beach Series.

www.avca.org—The home page of the American Volleyball Coaches Association (AVCA). Information on the latest in volleyball coaching, sport science and sports medicine education for coaching and athlete development, and national publications and convention educational opportunities is available.

Newsgroups:
rec.sport.volleyball—Information that is posted and read free of charge is located at this site. News changes weekly.

Email:
Info@usav.org—General information about volleyball can be obtained.

Intern@usav.org—Internship opportunities for undergraduate and master's degree students in sport administration through USA Volleyball

Firstname.lastname@usav.org—To reach a USA Volleyball's staff member or someone on its Board of Directors, use this format.

VIDEOS

(Available from American Volleyball Coaches Association, www.avca.org)
Blueprint for designing volleyball practices by Mike Hebert, University of Minnesota
Setter training and team warmup by Mike Hebert, University of Minnesota
Gold Medal Volleyball by Pat Powers
World of volleyball
Volleyball—The keys to success
Beach volleyball—Get involved
USA Volleyball Guide to Athlete Conditioning, USA Volleyball
Back row attack by Mary Wise, University of Florida
Ball handling drills by Patty Dowdell, Texas Woman's University
Fundamental skills for volleyball by Megan Clayberg, Central College
Spiking: Step by step development by Brian Gimmillaro, Long Beach State University

Attacking by Kathy DeBoer, University of Kentucky
Blocking by Don Shaw, Stanford University
Passing by Don Shaw, Stanford University
Individual defense by Kathy DeBoer, University of Kentucky
Serve and serve receive drills by Kathy DeBoer, University of Kentucky
Transition drills by Andy Banachowski, UCLA
Strength and power training
Japan elementary school championship video I and II
AVCA statistics video and manual
Scorekeeper's video
Line judge video
College recruiting—Make it happen workbook and video
Technical evaluation—Atlanta 1996
Skills, kills and drills

ORGANIZATIONS

USA Volleyball (USAV)
715 So. Circle Drive
Colorado Springs, CO 80910-2368
Information about club, youth, national team, coaching education, volleyball rules,
Olympic volleyball.
Email: Info@usav.org
Toll free information line: 1-88USVOLLEY

American Volleyball Coaches Association (AVCA)
1227 Lake Plaza Drive
Suite B
Colorado Springs, CO 80906
Email: svivas@avca.org
Phone: 719-576-7777
Fax back service: 719-576-7778
Weekly results and poll line: 719-576-7798

Federation Nationale de Volleyball (FIVB)
Avenue de la Gare 12
CH—1003 LAUSANNE
Switzerland
Email: www.fivb.org

National Association for Girls and Women in Sport (NAGWS)
Information about collegiate women's volleyball rules
1900 Association Drive
Reston, VA 21091
Email: deverett@aahperd.org

Professional Association of Volleyball Officials (PAVO)
PO Box 8660
Topeka, KS 66608
1-888-791-2074

USEFUL ACRONYMS

USA Volleyball—The new name for the United States Volleyball Association (USVBA) since 1994
USAV—USA Volleyball
BOD—Board of Directors
RVA—Regional Volleyball Association

USA Volleyball Divisions:
MRHR—Member Relations and Human Resources Division of USA Volleyball
NCD—National Championship Division of USA Volleyball
OD—Officials Division of USA Volleyball
ROD—Regional Operations Division of USA Volleyball
YJOV—Youth/Junior Olympic Division of USA Volleyball
Disabled
Beach

Member Organizations of USA Volleyball:
AAHPERD—American Alliance for Health, Physical Education, Recreation, and Dance
AAU—Amateur Athletic Union
ABO—see PAVO
ADVA—American Deaf Volleyball Association
AIA—Athletes in Action
American Turners—no acronym
AVCA—American Volleyball Coaches Association
AVP—Association of Volleyball Professionals
BSA—Boy Scouts of America
CBVA—California Beach Volleyball Association
DSUSA—Disabled Sports USA
GSUSA—Girls Scouts USA
JCC—Jewish Community Centers
NAIA—National Association of Intercollegiate Athletics
NAPAL—National Association of Police Athletic Leagues
NCAA—National Collegiate Athletic Association
NCSG—National Congress of State Games
NFSHSA—National Federation of State High School Associations
NIRSA—National Intramural Recreational Sports Association
NJCAA—National Junior College Athletic Association
NRPA—National Recreation and Parks Association
PAVO—Professional Association of Volleyball Officials

PCPFS—President's Council on Physical Fitness and Sports
SOI—Special Olympics International
USAF—United States Air Force
USAFA—United States Air Force Academy
USMC—United States Marine Corps
USN—United States Navy
VBHF—Volleyball Hall of Fame
WI—Wallyball International, Inc.
WGMF—William G. Morgan Foundation

Others:
FIVB—Federation Internationale de Volleyball
IOC—International Olympic Committee
NGB—National Governing Body of Sport
OTC—United States Olympic Training Center
USOC—United States Olympic Committee

Appendix C

[Portions taken from: Kluka, D. A., & Planer, P. A. (1998). Improving volleyball decision making through visual/perceptual skills training, *Performance Conditioning for Volleyball, 6*(2), 7–8.]

Increasing evidence suggests that volleyball skill acquisition has at least three components for success: (1) information gathered by the player through the visual system; (2) perceptual decision-making strategies developed through the visual system/brain connection, and (3) efficient and effective movement production resulting from the visual system/brain/body connection.

According to volleyball researchers, there are also at least nine factors which contribute to the lack of performance success. Of these, several involve the visual/perceptual system and decision making: (1) lack of recognition (reading); (2) late reading; (3) lack of inner focus for accuracy; and (4) poor selection of inner options.

It should be no surprise that visual/perceptual skills play a primary role in the quest for volleyball excellence. Generally, there is a core of visual/perceptual skills needed to optimize success in volleyball: (1) acuity (dynamic/static), (2) vergence (convergence/divergence), (3) dynamic stereopsis, (4) central/peripheral awareness, (5) glare recovery, (6) contrast sensitivity function, (7) fusion, (8) color perception, (9) and total reaction time. These skills, when integrated with a quick action plan, provide volleyball players with the ability to determine what will likely occur before the ball is in play and to react most efficiently and effectively when it is.

Each player should have the sharpest static visual acuity possible. Sharp static visual acuity can be attained through the use of spectacles or contact lenses if necessary. Players should have vision evaluated at least once every two years by a sports vision optometrist or ophthalmologist.

VISUAL SKILLS ENHANCEMENT EXERCISES*

Because accommodation and convergence, dynamic visual acuity, dynamic stereopsis, peripheral vision, and speed and span of recognition can be improved through practice, the following exercises may also help enhance visual skills needed to improve volleyball performance.

*Adapted from Revien & Gabor, 1981, and Kluka & Love, 1989.

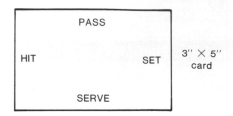

Example of an accommodation and convergence index card. Adapted from Revien & Gabor, 1981, and Kluka & Love, 1989.

Accommodation and convergence. Courtesy of D. Kluka

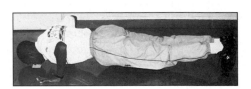

Accommodation and convergence.

ACCOMMODATION AND CONVERGENCE

▶ Equipment

3" × 5" (7.62 × 12.7 cm) card. Place four volleyball-related terms on the card. Place the card in the line of sight while in the pushup position.

▶ Exercise

20 pushups: Focus on one word on the card. Perform twenty pushups, moving from approximately 15 inches (40 cm) to the near point of convergence. Keep each word on the card looking like a single word as long as possible. Change the focus between the four words, moving the eyes in a clockwise manner.

DYNAMIC VISUAL ACUITY

▶ Equipment

Mini trampoline, 24" × 26" (60.96 × 91.44 cm) posterboard. Mount the posterboard to a wall ten feet (3.048 m) away at eye level when standing on the mini tramp.

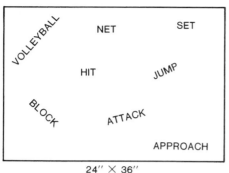

24″ × 36″
Posterboard

Example of a posterboard used with the minitramp.

Dynamic visual acuity.
Courtesy of D. Kluka

▶ **Exercise**

Bounce on the mini tramp; read the words as rapidly as possible in a variety of sequences. Practice for two one-minute sessions, resting one minute. For variation, place three-letter words on three bean bags. As you bounce, have someone toss the bean bags into the air. Read the words as rapidly as possible.

DEPTH PERCEPTION

▶ **Equipment**

Two one-inch buttons, two screw eyes, twenty-five feet (7.62 m) of heavy string, one piece of 15″ × ¾″ × 3″ (38.1 × 1.905 × 7.62 cm) plywood, hammer, nails, hand drill. At eye level, nail the plywood onto the wall. Screw the two screw eyes into the plywood so that they are in a straight horizontal line, six inches (15.24 cm) apart. Insert the string through both screw eyes, one at a time. Pull the string ends until they are even, creating approximately twelve feet (3.66 m) on each side. Slide one button onto the left end of the string so that its position remains seven feet (21.13 m) from the end. It may be necessary to place a knot before and after the button if it slides easily along the string. Perform a similar procedure with the second button on the right side of the string, securely positioning it at five feet (1.524 m).

▶ **Exercise**

Stand approximately twelve feet (3.66 m) from the wall, holding each end of the string in the corresponding hand so that the hands are at eye level. With both eyes

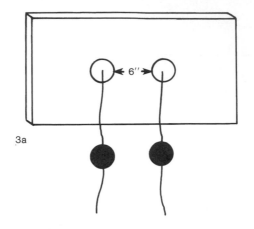

3a

Example of the board used with
dynamic stereopsis.

Depth perception.
Courtesy of D. Kluka

Depth perception.

open, push and pull the string until both buttons are believed to be aligned. After releasing both ends of the string, measure the distance the buttons are out of alignment. If the distance is larger than one inch (2.54 cm), the buttons should be set closer to the wall (nine and eleven feet [2.74 and 3.35 m]). Practice for three-minute sessions, changing the right/left button locations so that the left button is in front of the right one an equal amount of time.

PERIPHERAL AWARENESS

▶ Equipment

VCR player, television, videotape of any volleyball match, straight-back chair, pencil with an eraser.

Peripheral awareness.
Courtesy of D. Kluka

Peripheral awareness.

▶ Exercise

Sit directly in front of the television screen in a straight-back chair with the line of vision approximately six feet (1.83 m) from the screen. While the videotaped volleyball match is playing, hold the pencil vertically at arm's length and focus upon the pencil's eraser. Focus for two thirty-second intervals, allowing one minute rest. As focusing ability improves, describe what you are seeing peripherally.

SPEED AND SPAN OF RECOGNITION

▶ Equipment

One deck of playing cards, one black permanent marking pen. Place a black dot, ¼ inch (.64 cm) in diameter in the center of the top of each card.

▶ Exercise

Hold the deck of cards approximately fifteen inches (38.10 cm) away and at eye level, focusing on the black dot. The cards are slowly flipped by holding them from the bottom in one hand and bending the deck back with the thumb of the other hand. The rate of flipping is determined by quickness in mental identification of each number. To

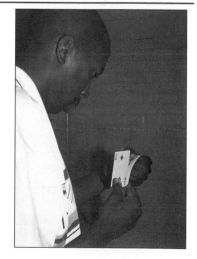

Speed and span of recognition.
Courtesy of D. Kluka

increase the span of recognition, place a different number or letter in the upper right-hand corner of each playing card. Practice for two two-minute time intervals.

VISUAL SKILLS CONSIDERATIONS

The eyes play an indispensable role when playing the game of volleyball. Fundamentally, the sense of vision is similar to other senses. The eye's retina encodes the visual world. It transforms optical images into trains of nerve impulses, which are then conducted along the optic nerve to the brain. The brain interprets those signals to generate visual perception: a subjective sense of shapes, colors, and movements that surround the volleyball player. The ability to appropriately interpret what is perceived is learned, just as other skill related to volleyball are learned.

Rapidly changing information characterizes the environment of the volleyball player. The player must quickly and continuously select from an almost overwhelming amount of visual information in order to perform successfully.

Appropriate interpretation depends upon the development of several visual skills:

1. convergence
2. accommodation
3. dynamic visual acuity
4. depth perception
5. peripheral vision
6. speed and span of recognition

Having two eyes makes possible binocular, or stereoscopic, vision. During serve reception, two images of the server are received from slightly different angles, giving the impression of distance and depth; this adds a third dimension to the visual world.

Convergence of the eyes takes place by contraction of the extrinsic eye muscles. Both eyeballs move inwardly once the ball is served so the eyes come together, or converge, toward the ball. The closer the ball gets, the greater the degree of convergence necessary to maintain single vision.

The ability to change focus in viewing the ball clearly at near and far distances can be termed accommodation. The relationship of convergence and accommodation is particularly important during serve reception. When the ball is served, the receiver views its direction, speed, and distance. The farther away the ball is, the less three-dimensional it appears. As the ball approaches, more convergence is necessary to maintain focus on the ball to forearm contact.

Acuity is the sharpness of vision and the degree of detail the brain can interpret when looking at an object. The object can be either stationary (static) or moving (dynamic). Static visual acuity (SVA) can be measured with the Snellen Eye Chart and is reported as 20/20, 20/30, or 20/40. It is two-dimensional. If SVA is blurred, it becomes difficult for the player to accurately focus before serving the ball to a specific target.

Dynamic visual acuity (DVA) refers to the capacity to discriminate a specific object from background when there is relative movement between the player and the object. Depth perception, giving a three-dimensionality to the world, plays an integral role in DVA. If the discrimination of a moving ball is diminished, the receiver may integrate information inappropriate for the execution of a successful pass.

The ability to quickly and accurately judge the distance between the player and the ball is based upon depth perception. Depth perception is dependent upon both eyes working together simultaneously. It may be critical to the middle back who must quickly and accurately judge a ball just hit by the opposing team's strong side hitter.

Peripheral vision enables the player to maintain an awareness of what is happening outside the direct line of vision. The center of vision is maintained on the ball. A setter may rely heavily upon the use of peripheral vision. While focusing on the approaching ball, the setter must also be able to see what is occurring with the attacker being set as well as viewing the formation of the block and other defensive players.

Speed and span of recognition involves how quickly and accurately something can be distinguished. The larger the span of recognition, the less head movement involved. If the player can interpret important movements with a larger span of vision, there will be less head movement. It is important for the attacker to be able to view the ball as it is set, the block as it forms, and the placement of other defensive players as they dig into their positions. The less head movement involved for the attacker, the more intent the focus can be.

Because the game of volleyball has a rapidly changing environment, the player must quickly and continuously select relevant visual cues. While learning volleyball skills, consider learning from the "eyes down." Visual skills enhancement exercises can facilitate our ability to make quicker decisions for action.

Assessment C-1

Name   Section   Date

Equipment: One volleyball. Place a variety of different colored dots (no more than 1 inch in diameter) on each of the panels of the volleyball.

Activity: The athlete, upon contact with the ball, calls out the color that the right or left hand was in contact with. Before the drill, the decisions of which hand to call can be made. To make the drill more difficult, the hand can be called two seconds before ball contact.

Add difficulty: Place three dots per panel (no more than ½ inch in diameter) on every other panel of the volleyball. Using little or no spin, toss the ball to the player in a game-like situation (e.g., to the setter, to the receiver, to the blocker, or to the hitter) to see how quickly the player can discern the number of dots viewed.

Add difficulty: Increase the spin on the ball during the toss.

Assessment C-2

Name   Section   Date

Equipment: Net, two flashlights, two assistants, volleyballs. Place a dot (no larger than one inch in diameter and in contrasting color to the white top of the net) at the top portion of the net. This dot serves as the central dot. Place four other dots (no larger than one inch in diameter, in contrasting colors to the black net, and two on each side of the central dot) in various positions along the net to simulate blocking angles.

Activity: From a blocking position, the player jumps and blocks the appropriate angle as simulated by the dots when both the central and peripheral dot are highlighted. Working together, two assistants serve as highlighters. One shines the beam of the flashlight on the primary dot. The second highlights another dot (the peripheral dot) with a second flashlight. On some occasions, the central dot will be highlighted while at other times it will not. The assistant who is lighting the peripheral dots keeps one highlighted while at other times not. The player must attend to both the central and peripheral dots at the same time.

Add difficulty: Move the peripheral dots farther apart.

Assessment C-3

Name   Section   Date

Equipment: One assistant, tachistoscope, overhead projector or slide projector.

Activity: Have a predetermined action for the player to perform whenever a certain sequences is flashed on the front wall. These could be symbols representing particular offensive plays that will be run by the team. Set the duration of exposure so that the player is relatively successful in viewing the flashed information. For example, whenever a "4" is flashed on the wall, the player moves to a free-ball position; whenever a "3" is flashed, the player moves to block.

Add difficulty: Decrease the viewing time and/or increase the complexity of the symbols used.

Appendix D

USA Volleyball is the National Governing Body (NGB) for the sport in the United States. Because of its position within the Olympic Movement, it is important to understand the depth and breadth of the organization. Appendix D illustrates, in chart form, the structure of USA Volleyball and the vast opportunities it provides those interested in being associated with the game. Membership in USA Volleyball can be attained through Regional Organization (e.g., Great Lakes Region, Lone Star Region, Southern Region) involvement or one of its numerous Member Organizations (e.g., YMCA, NCAA, American Turners).

In order to better understand opportunities available to play the game of volleyball, USA Volleyball has developed an Athlete Pipeline model that graphically depicts how a player can become an Olympic or professional player. For further details, contact the USA Volleyball Office, Colorado Springs, Colorado.

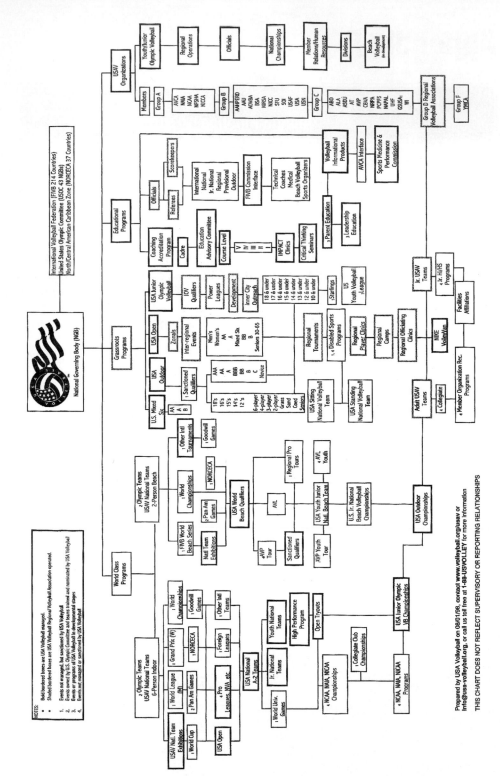

ATHLETE PIPELINE
*"Success at the highest level depends on
the strength of the entire pipeline..."*

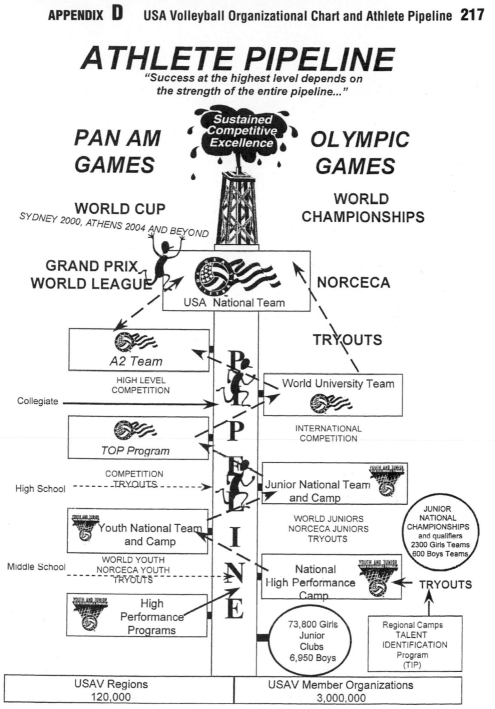

Appendix E

1896 Volleyball Rules

The game of volleyball has recently passed the century mark. The original rules, published here, serve as the benchmark for over a century of growth and development of the sport.

PREFACE

As the game of volleyball celebrates its centennial anniversary, the Rules of the Game Commission would like to share with all those who now participate in the sport the original rules for the game of volleyball as created by Mr. W. G. Morgan. These rules, when compared with those for 2000, illustrate the evolution of the sport of volleyball.

VOLLEYBALL

During the past winter, Mr. W. G. Morgan of Holyoke, Mass, has developed a game in his gymnasium which is called Volley Ball. It was presented at the Physical Directors' Conference, and the general impression seemed to be that it would fill a place not filled by any other game. It is to be played indoors, and by those who wish a game not so rough as basketball and yet one in which the same degree of activity is demanded. The complete report as given to the Conference by W. G. Morgan is as follows:

* * *

Volleyball is a new game which is preeminently fitted for the gymnasium or the exercise hall, but which may be played out of doors. Any number of persons may play the game. The play consists of keeping a ball in motion over a high net, from one side to the other, thus partaking of the character of two games, tennis and hand ball.

Play is started by a player on one side serving the ball over the net into the opponents' field or court. The opponents then, without allowing the ball to strike the floor, return it, and it is in this way kept going back and forth until one side fails to return it or it hits the floor. This counts a "score" for one side or a "server out" for the other depending upon the side in point. The game consists of nine innings, each side serving a certain number of times, as per rules, in each inning.*

RULES OF VOLLEYBALL

1. GAME. The game consists of nine innings.
2. INNING. An inning consists of when one person is playing on each side, one service on each side; when two are playing on each side, two services on each side; when three or more are playing on each side, three services on each side. The man serving continues to do so until out by failure of his side to return the ball. Each man shall serve in turn.
3. COURT. The court of floor space shall be twenty-five feet wide and fifty feet long, to be divided into two square courts, twenty-five by twenty-five feet, by the net. Four feet from the net on either side and parallel with it shall be a line across the court, the Dribbling line. The boundary lines must be plainly marked so as to be visible from all parts of the courts.
   Note—The exact size of the court may be changed to suit the convenience of the place.
4. NET. The net shall be at least two feet wide and twenty-seven feet long, and shall be suspended from uprights placed at least one foot outside the side lines. The TOP LINE of the net must be six feet six inches from the floor.
5. BALL. The ball shall be a rubber bladder covered with leather or canvas. It shall measure not less than twenty-five inches nor more than twenty-seven inches in circumference, and shall weigh not less than nine ounces nor more than twelve ounces.
6. SERVER AND SERVICE. The server shall stand with one foot on the back line. The ball must be batted with the hand. Two services or trials are allowed him to place the ball in the opponent's court (as in tennis). The server may serve into the opponent's court at any place. In a service the ball must be batted at least ten feet, no dribbling allowed. A service which would strike the net, but is struck by another of the same side before striking the net, if it goes over into the opponents' court is good, but if it should go outside, the server has no second trial.
7. SCORING. Each good service unreturned or ball in play unreturned by the side receiving, counts one score for the side serving. A side only scores when serving, as a failure to return the ball on their part results in the server being put out.
8. NET BALL. A play which hits the net aside from the first service is called a net ball and is equivalent to a failure to return, counting for the opposite side. The ball hitting the net on first service shall be called *dead*, and counts as a trial.

*Adapted from "A Summary of Seventy-Five Years of Rules" by William T. Odneal, which appeared in the 1970 *Annual Official Volleyball Rules and Reference Guide of the United States Volleyball Association* and again in the 1995 edition.

9. LINE BALL. It is a ball striking the boundary line: it is equivalent to one out of court and counts as such.
10. PLAY AND PLAYERS. Any number may play that is convenient to the place. A player should be able to cover about ten by ten feet.

Should any player during play touch the net, it puts the ball out of play and counts against his side. Should any player catch or hold for an instant the ball, it is out of play and counts for the opposite side. Should the ball strike any object other than the floor and bound back into the court, it is still in play.

To DRIBBLE the ball is to carry it all the time keeping it bouncing. When dribbling the ball no player shall cross the Dribbling line, this putting the ball out of play and counting against him.

Any player, except the captain, addressing the umpire or casting any slurring remarks at him or any of the players on the opposite side, may be disqualified and his side be compelled to play the game without him or a substitute or forfeit the game.

HELPS IN PLAYING THE GAME

Strike the ball with both hands.
Look for uncovered space in opponents' field.

Play together: cover your own space.
Pass from one to another when possible.
Watch the play constantly, especially the opponents'.

Reference: Morgan WG. Rules of Volleyball. Physical Ed (July) 1896; 50–1.

GLOSSARY

A

ACCOMMODATION   A visual skill used in volleyball; the ability to change focus instantly and smoothly throughout points in space.

ACE   A served ball that leads directly to a point for the serving team.

AEROBIC/ANAEROBIC   Types of energy systems used by the body; the former uses oxygen, the latter does not require oxygen.

AGILITY   The ability to change directions quickly.

AIAW   Association of Intercollegiate Athletics for Women; initiated the first women's national collegiate championships.

ATTACK   The attempt by the offensive team to end play by hitting the ball to the floor of the defensive team; high-speed, medium speed, slow speed.

ATTACK BLOCK   A play that serves to angle the ball down onto the opponents' side of the court after it is contacted by an attacker.

ATTACK COVERAGE   As play develops, the opposing team adjusts its defense to defend the ensuing attack by covering the attacker and the court.

ATTACK LINE   Line on the court parallel to the net and 3 m (10 ft) away from it.

ATTACKER   A team player who spikes the ball in a downward trajectory (usually the team's final hit in the offensive play). Also referred to as a hitter or spiker.

AUDIBLE OFFENSE   To verbalize a set or play pattern.

B

BACK ROW ATTACK   Offensive attack generated by back row player from behind the attack line.

BACK SLIDE ATTACK   Player takes off from one foot and is moving the same direction as the ball.

BACK ZONE   Area that is delimited by attack line and endline.

BACK ZONE PLAYER   A team member who has position 1, 5, or 6 in the rotational order. The player may not jump to attack on or in front of the 3 m line when the ball is completely above the top of the net and may not participate in a block.

BLOCK   One, two, or three defensive players jumping in front of an attacker to prevent or slow down a spiked ball hit from the attack. Generally, the ball is contacted with the hands.

BLOCKER(S)   The team player(s) responsible for blocking the attack. They may only be players in rotational positions 2, 3, and/or 4 (front row).

BODY LINE   An imaginary line that runs from the top of the head through the base of the feet, bisecting the body vertically so two equal halves are formed.

BUMP   An outdated or colloquial term meaning forearm pass.

C

COMMIT BLOCK   Plan made in advance to block a predetermined hitter.

CONTROL BLOCK   An attempted block that slows down the speed of an attack so the back row players have an opportunity to play the ball.

CONVERGENCE   A visual skill used in the game of volleyball. The eyes focus on one point in space at a time.

COOL DOWN   Gradually decreasing the intensity of an activity and preparing the body for normal daily activity.

CROSSCOURT   An attack generated at an angle from one side of the attacking team's court to the opposite side of the defending team's court.

D

DEPTH PERCEPTION   (dynamic stereopsis) A visual skill used in volleyball; the ability to judge the distance of objects.

DIG   Using a forearm or hand pass to play a ball that is in a low movement zone as a result of a hard hit attack.

DINK   See **Tipping.**

DIVE   An emergency technique used when a player must extend the range of effectiveness. The player contacts the ball and then lands on the chest, abdomen, and thighs.

DOWN BALL   An attacked ball that the blockers judge as lacking sufficient speed to require a block. The blockers shout "down ball" so that other team players can move to pass the ball to convert it into their offensive play.

DRIFTING   Unnecessarily shifting the body laterally during takeoff in an airborne movement.

DUMP   Instead of setting the ball, the offensive player dinks the ball over the net.

DYNAMIC BALANCE   Performing a movement in space that is in control; adjusting the body's center of mass through the movement.

DYNAMIC STEREOPSIS   See Depth Perception.

DYNAMIC VISUAL ACUITY   The ability to see sharply and clearly an object/person when the object/person and/or you are in motion.

E

EMERGENCY TECHNIQUE   A method to retrieve a ball that is outside the player's range of effectiveness. Examples include a dive and catch, an extension roll, or a dive and slide.

ENDLINES   Boundaries of the court on either end.

ENDURANCE   The ability to perform a muscular movement repeatedly without fatigue.

EXTENSION ROLL   An emergency technique where the ball is contacted in a low movement zone and out of body line. The result of contacting the ball out of body line is a roll that thrusts the feet over the shoulders so that the player is returned to the feet. Also referred to as a Japanese roll.

F

FIVB (FEDERATION INTERNATIONALE DE VOLLEYBALL)   The FIVB governs international volleyball play and represents the sport of volleyball on the International Olympic Committee (IOC).

FLEXIBILITY   Range of motion within joints of the human body.

FLOATER SERVE   A method of putting the ball into play. The ball, once served with an overarm movement pattern, has little or no spin, thereby creating a "wiggling" effect through the air as it approaches the serve receiver.

FOOT PLANT   Placing of the feet at takeoff during an attack.

FOREARM PASS   One of the basic skills in the game of volleyball. Any ball arriving at or below the player's waist can be easily passed using the forearms as the contacting surface.

FREE BALL   A ball returned by the opposing team that has little speed and high trajectory and can be played easily by the back row in order to set up a team attack.

FRONT ZONE   Area delimited by center line and attack line.

FRONT ZONE PLAYER   A team member who has rotational position 2, 3, or 4 in the rotational order.

H

HIGH SEAM   An intentional attack of the ball between the hands of two blockers.

HIT   See **Attack.**

HITTER   See **Attacker.**

J

JAPANESE ROLL   See **Extension Roll.**

JOUST   Ball held between two players above net; play continues.

JUMP SERVE   Produces angular velocities in excess of 23 m/s.

JUMP SET   Setter becomes airborne to meet the pass in order to reduce the time it takes for the ball to get from setter to attacker.

L

LIBERO PLAYER   A defensive specialist who may substitute for any back court player.

LINE ZONE   Zone 5, with little time to react defensively.

M

METABOLIC SPECIFICITY TRAINING   Training the energy systems used by the body according to the metabolic demand of the sport.

MOVEMENT ZONES   Four basic areas of movement needed for movement in the game of volleyball: airborne, high, medium, and low.

MULTIPLE BLOCK   Two or three players participating in the blocking attempt.

MULTIPLE OFFENSIVE SYSTEM   Playing system that uses a setter from the back court and permits attackers in the front zone.

MUSCULAR POWER   Ability to generate a maximum force in the shortest amount of time.

MUSCULAR STRENGTH   The ability to perform a movement maximally at any one time

N

NATIONAL ASSOCIATION FOR GIRLS AND WOMEN IN SPORT (NAGWS)   An association within the American Alliance for Health, Physical Education, Recreation, and Dance (AAHPERD). It writes the intercollegiate women's volleyball rules and provides paths for advocacy recruitment, and enhancement of females in sport and sport leadership positions.

NATIONAL COLLEGIATE ATHLETIC ASSOCIATION (NCAA)   An organization that administers men's and women's intercollegiate athletic programs in three divisions.

NATIONAL GOVERNING BODY (NGB)   A body composed of amateur sport organizations that are represented on the United States Olympic Committee (USOC). USA volleyball represents the sport of volleyball on the USOC.

NEUROMUSCULAR SPECIFICITY TRAINING   Training the muscles actually used to play the game by simulating game like situations.

O

OFFENSIVE SYSTEM   A team's attack system that promotes the use of the team's strengths in specific situations; examples include 4–2; 5–1; 6–2.

OFF-HAND SIDE OF THE COURT   See option side.

OFFICIATING TEAM   First referee, second referee, two or four line judges, scorekeeper.

OFF-SPEED ATTACK   A spiked ball that has topspin but less than its maximum force.

OPENING THE PASSING LANES   As the served ball travels toward the net, the potential passers face the ball. As the ball passes over the net, all players not directly involved with the pass pivot and open toward the passer.

OPTION SIDE OF THE COURT   Right side when the attacker is right-handed.

OUTSIDE BLOCKER   Player in LF or RF position who sets this block.

OVERHEAD PASS   One of the basic volleyball skills whereby a player contacts the ball with both hands simultaneously to control it and allow for continuation of the team's attack play.

OVERLAP   A ruling based on foot placement of members of the receiving team as a ball is served. Adjacent players must keep their feet from completely crossing an imaginary dividing line, which would allow an unfair advantage for their team.

P

PASS   The first of 3 contacts which can be overhead or forearm.

PERIPHERAL VISION   A visual skill used in volleyball. The width of the visual field and awareness of what is going on while focusing straight ahead.

PLAYER-BACK DEFENSE   One of the back row players drops back to the endline while the two other back row side players move to their respective side lines.

PLAYING AREA   Front, back, free substitution, and serving zones.

POINTS   The method of keeping score; one point is scored per designated result according to the rules.

POWER   The ability to perform maximally at a rapid rate.

$$\text{Power} = \frac{\text{force} \times \text{distance}}{\text{time}}.$$

POWER SIDE OF THE COURT   Left side when the attacker is right handed.

Q

QUICK ATTACK   An attack that is usually generated from the middle after a very short set.

R

RALLY   The time from the serve initiation until play is ended by a point or sideout.

RALLY SCORING   A point is scored when either team wins the rally.

RANGE OF EFFECTIVENESS   Each player has a limited area on the court that can be easily reached. It extends in approximately a four-foot radius from the player's ready position.

READING   Watching opposite players' movements to make decisions about court offense or defense.

READY POSITION   A position that is comfortable and balanced for the player to move from quickly in order to play a ball.

RED CARD   A severe sanction given by the first referee.

REPETITIONS   The number of times an exercise is completed.

ROOFING THE BALL   Ball is completely covered by the blocker.

ROTATIONAL ORDER   The right back position is considered as 1, right front is 2, middle front is 3, left front is 4, left back is 5, and middle back is 6. The rotational order must be maintained at the time the ball is contacted for service.

S

SCOREBOARD   Visible scorekeeping device for the match.

SEAM   An area where there is weakness or no coverage.

SERVE   One of the basic volleyball skills. It is used to begin a game or put the ball in play.

SERVE RECEIVE   A forearm pass generally used to direct the ball to the setter for the team's attack.

SERVICE ZONE   Area located behind each end line.

SERVING ORDER   See **Rotational Order.**

SERVING STRATEGY   Predetermined manner of how, when and where the ball will be served to gain an advantage.

SET   The overhead pass used as an offensive skill to direct the ball to an area where an attacker can contact the ball for the team's attack.

SETTER   The player who is designated to organize and execute the teams offensive play.

SETTER ATTACK   Returning the ball over the net on the first or second contact.

SETTING OPTIONS   Offensive plays used by the setter to facilitate the team's offense.

SIDE BANDS   While, vertical bands on the net.

SIDE LINES   Boundaries of the court on either side.

SIDE OUT   When the serving team loses the ball after a rally, the receiving team gets the ball. The result of this transition is a sideout and point.

SITTING VOLLEYBALL   Teams of players who play from a seated position with rule modifications; part of Disabled volleyball.

SKIP/JUMP   A foot pattern that assists in moving a player quickly to a statically balanced position in order to play the ball when using a forearm pass.

SLIDE ATTACK   An attack designed to confuse blockers with numerous possibilities.

SPECIALIZATION   Player has particular responsibilities.

SPECIAL OLYMPICS UNIFIED VOLLEYBALL   Teams which include special Olympians and partners.

SPECIFICITY OF TRAINING   Training the body through movements that simulate movements used in a specific sport.

SPEED AND SPAN OF RECOGNITION   Visual skills used in volleyball. The speed and amount of information perceived and/or the extent of information recognized within a specific context.

SPIKE   See **Attack.**

SPIKER   See **Attacker.**

SPLIT-THE-BLOCK   Back zone defensive player places the center of the body in a line between two blockers.

SPRAWL   An emergency technique used when the player has reached completely forward and must extend parallel to the floor to play the ball.

STANDING VOLLEYBALL   Teams composed of specified number of points resulting from appendage loss; part of disabled sports.

STRESS ADAPTATION PRINCIPLE   When the body is under physical stress, it changes or adapts to that stress.

SUBSTITUTE   Player who enters the game after the game has begun.

SUBSTITUTION ZONE   Area that is an imaginary extension of attack lines including officials' table.

SUPPORTIVE MOVEMENT   Movement by players who are not directly involved in playing the ball but, by body movement, assist in team communication.

SWITCHING   As soon as the serve is contacted, players on the court may exchange positions, thereby moving into positions that best suit the offensive dynamics of their team. However, rotational position 2, 3, or 4 determines who can attack or block in accordance with the rules.

T

TECHNIQUE   How the ball is played.

TEMPO   Directing the ball at varying speeds and heights to facilitate the attack beating the block.

TIPPING   An off-speed attack in which the attacker gently places the ball behind or around the block. Also called **Dink.**

TOOLING THE BLOCK   Using the block to cause the ball to go out of bounds during an attack.

TOP SPIN SERVE   Top spin at contact and holds ball on course.

TRADITIONAL OFFENSIVE SYSTEM   Playing system that uses two attackers and one setter in the front court.

TRAJECTORY   Once airborne, the path of the body or the ball.

TRANSITION   Adjustment from one phase of the play to another, as in defense to offense.

U

UNDERHAND SERVE   Using an underhand movement pattern, the ball may be put into play. Usually used with young players.

UNITED STATES OLYMPIC COMMITTEE (USOC)   An administrative organization that represents amateur sport throughout the United States. Internationally, the USOC represents the United States as a member of the International Olympic Committee (IOC).

UNITED STATES VOLLEYBALL ASSOCIATION (USVBA)   The national governing body for the sport of volleyball in the United States. Also know as USA Volleyball.

USA VOLLEYBALL (USAV)   See **United States Volleyball Association (USVBA).**

W

"W" PATTERN   A five-player service reception pattern; their court positions resemble the letter "W."

WARMUP   Increasing blood flow to muscles through large movements using major muscle groups.

WARMUP AREA   Area located even with, but not beyond the bench.

WASH DRILLS   The teacher/coach adds one or more balls to the game. The object of the drill is for the players to learn how to focus on the existing ball to clear it off the court while anticipating the next ball. Points can be added for successfully playing a ball to completion; points can be subtracted for unsuccessful performance (like washing out).

WIPING THE BLOCK   An attacking technique that results in the ball rebounding out of the court off of the blockers' hands.

Y

YELLOW CARD   Warning given by the first referee.

Z

ZONE OF REST   Zone 6, with the ball entering the deep area of the court defensively.

INDEX